Independents
Declared

D1713426

The Dilemmas of Independent Trucking

Independents Declared

SMITHSONIAN SERIES IN ETHNOGRAPHIC INQUIRY

Michael H. Agar

SMITHSONIAN INSTITUTION PRESS
Washington, D.C.   London

∞™ The paper in this book meets the guidelines for permanence and
durability of the Committee on Production Guidelines for Book
Longevity of the Council on Library Resources.

Library of Congress Cataloging in Publication Data
Agar, Michael H.
Independents Declared
(Smithsonian series in ethnographic inquiry; v. 4)
Bibliography: p. 186
Includes index.
    1. Trucking—United States. I. Title. II. Series.
HE5623.A525   1986   388.3′24′0973 85-43243
ISBN 0-87474-250-1 (cloth)
ISBN 0-87474-251-X (pap.)

Edited by Michelle Smith
Designed by Christopher Jones
Cover: Photograph by Jeff Ploskonka, Division of Transportation,
National Museum of American History, Smithsonian Institution,
Washington, D.C.

Table of Contents

Acknowledgments

By the ethics of anthropological research, the people I interviewed are supposed to have pseudonyms. They do, but many of them would prefer that I used their real names. Since I can't, I would like to thank, anonymously, the owner-operators, their family members, and other people involved in trucking who gave generously of their time and knowledge to educate a naive outsider. When I think back to the first days of the research, it amazes me how easy it is to think you know what the trucking industry is all about from the outside, and how wrong you are once you learn it from the inside.

Over the long haul of converting piles of transcripts into a book, several people helped. Thomas Corsi of the College of Business and Management got me started with his papers and advice, discussed my work as it went along, and provided a valuable critique of the manuscript. Rita Bontz, president of the Maryland Independent Truckers and Drivers Association (MITDA), introduced me to the world of independent trucking, and to people who taught me their view of the industry, and also guided me through the research and critiqued the manuscript. Those two were the mainstays.

Most of the research was done with the help of members of MITDA. They talked to me, took me on trips, explained issues during conversations at meetings, and invited me to their homes. They still do. And many other drivers took the time to chat over coffee in truck stops or cigarettes at loading docks. Several people from different parts of life read through the manuscript and gave me helpful comments. My kinfolk in Nevada City, California; my anthropological partners in Washington, Linda Bennett, Erve Chambers, and Jim MacDonald; Baltimore owner-operators Ted Brooks and Bob Bontz; Sara Bryant; a corporate executive with a major carrier; anthropologists Fred Gamst and Roger Sanjek; and Daniel Goodwin and Michelle Smith, the editors for Smithsonian. People who will read books in need of help and give it deserve a place in the altruism hall of fame.

Finally, in supporting roles, an NIH Career Award (DA00055) gave me the time to start the study. The University of Maryland provided some transcription help, most of it done by Roberta Albers. Lori Spier worked on the index, and Rosanna Farrell helped gather information for the update.

Insignificant though the gesture is in comparison to the energy invested in my work by these people, I thank them all.

Chapter 1

An American Contradiction

Independence Declared

Declarations of *independence* and systems for *control*—the contradiction has been part of the American fabric since the beginning. On the one hand, personal freedom available to anyone with the imagination and energy to pursue and defend it. On the other hand, rules, regulations, and powerful interests eliminating choices until all that remains is life according to someone else's design. We celebrate the former, scapegoat the latter, and get confused when the scapegoat is explained as a means to the celebrated end.

If ever a case existed to dramatize the contradiction, it is the American independent trucker. He serves as a contemporary symbol of traditional American independence; he himself views his working world as one in which he is being suffocated by the control of others; and he is angry and confused about the unfulfilled promise of deregulation, which to date has only amplified his sense of dependency on others.

He is not the first to be squeezed by a contradiction between cultural image and social reality. The American open-range cowboy of the nineteenth century was used in a similar way. In fact, the independent trucker is often described as the cultural descendant of the cowboy. The cowboy, like the independent trucker, personifies a national theme. In both cases, the created image showed that at least some among us embody the cultural ideal of unrestrained personal freedom. Inevitably, a closer look at the social reality of those who carry the image tarnishes it.

A recent exhibition at the Library of Congress tracked the cowboy's history (Taylor and Maar 1983). After the Civil War, the open-range cowboys were unglamorous cogs in the business of rounding up and moving cattle from Texas to the railheads in Kansas. Theirs was a working style based largely on that of the Mexican *vaquero*, a term that survives in English as *buckaroo* (Taylor 1983a). Cowboys were black, brown, and Indian as well as white, and more often than not they worked for a manager who represented absentee owners or contractors and actually organized the trail drive. They wore utilitarian clothes, engaged in long days of hard work, and ate boring and nutritionally deficient food. The cattle drive did have its epic qualities though—extremes of weather, river crossings, and stampedes, for instance.

In the space of about thirty years the cowboy became obsolete. Open-range cattle raising turned into a boom industry, expanding into the northern plains until the market was oversaturated. The railroads expanded to directly link urban markets to ranchlands. The winter of 1886 wiped out many of the cattle. And finally, as the industry reorganized and settlers moved into the West, barbed wire was increasingly used to enclose private lands. The core events of the traditional cowboy's work—roundups and cattle drives—had disappeared.

No sooner was the open-range cowboy obsolete than the process of image formation began. The country was changing from a rural agrarian society based on small family farms to one based on urban industrial capitalism. Waves of immigration from eastern and southern Europe bred a new form of national chauvinism. In a time of confusion and anxiety the mythic cowboy appeared, "manly, self-reliant, virtuous, competitive (but always fair), a free agent in the labor market, dependent only on his own skills for employment, and, above all, 100 percent Anglo Saxon . . ." (Taylor 1983b). The earlier image of the lawless, reckless, rowdy, and crude cowboy dropped back into history. The new image grew with novels like *The Virginian*, traveling shows like Buffalo Bill's, the illustrations of Remington, and the person of Teddy Roosevelt.

The cowboy story is a fascinating one that could go on and on. For now, the differences between the open-range cowboy's social reality and the cultural uses that were made of him after his extinction provide an eerily accurate preview of the current situation of American independent truckers. Quite recently they also became national symbols, often explicitly described as the cultural descendant of the cowboy. Born of the first trucking shutdown to protest fuel shortages in 1973, the image was developed in newspapers, novels, television, and movies. Like the cowboys' image, the truckers' arose at a time of national confusion, after the crises of the 1960s and early 1970s. The image may be fading, since the 1983 shutdown featured more violence than we now are willing to tolerate among our ideals—a change from the cowboys, who could literally get away with murder.

But the image is still with us, and much of it accents the continuity with the trail drive, replacing the cattle herd with a van full of freight. Like the trail drive, the cross-country truck trip can be an epic event, as incidents in the study will show. The independent trucker dresses like a cowboy. He controls horsepower instead of a horse. He operates without social ties, moving through challenging situations with a quiet self-reliance born of competence at what he does. He is the ultimate entrepreneur in the free market, working for whom he pleases when he pleases and making good money in the process. That's the cultural image.

The social and economic reality is different, and it is to an understanding of these differences that this book is dedicated. More so than the nineteenth-century cowboy, the independent trucker is enmeshed in webs of dependency. He depends on others for access to the freight he will carry, for the rates he will be paid for carrying it, and for the regulatory paperwork required by federal and state authorities. During an actual trip, he depends on *shippers*—those who provide the freight—and *customers*—those who receive it—for loading and unloading procedures and for more paperwork. A variety of federal, state, and local authorities have the power to inspect him, his truck, and his freight. And when the inevitable mechanical problems occur, he depends on road mechanics who may prey on his helplessness, far from home with a load of freight that must be delivered.

The purpose of this book is to learn the texture of the independent truckers' working world from the point of view of those who occupy it. The research on which the book is based was a quest for the keys that enable persons not of that world to better understand it. The quest explores detailed descriptions by independent truckers themselves. It also draws on observations I made on interstate trips, documents unearthed in the archives of the Interstate Commerce Commission, and recent novels that depict the popular image.

The results highlight a fundamental American contradiction—independence versus control—in the working world of those who are currently charged with its safekeeping. The independent trucker is indeed the descendant of the open-range cowboy, not only because both are charged with personifying traditional American values, but also because that personification is only tenuously related to the social realities of their working life. For the cowboy, the myth was only a historical lie. For the independent trucker, the myth is an injustice, for it conceals the political and economic forces that threaten a distinctive occupational role.

Humanscape Exploration

The style of research that underlies this book is deviant in the world of American social science. It is a style less devoted to scientific testing than to patterned learning. It is less concerned with control of the data than with apprehending the controls that operate in the world of others. When the guiding question is "who are those people and how do they live"—as it is here for independent truckers—this research style is most appropriate, for it is especially designed to explore the humanscapes of others.

Any number of tactics might guide this exploration. Those who move into a new neighborhood or take a new job or learn to use a new language develop a tactic without thinking much about it. But professional explorers must be self-conscious, because they explore as a means to the end of producing a public statement. Researchers are accountable for their method—the process by which they reach their conclusions. The great irony is that method is emphasized without absolute agreement on what the proper method is.

Those who cast their lot with traditional science say that human worlds should be explored in the same way as natural worlds: vary A and watch B while all other things remain equal. In human worlds you first must learn what the As and Bs are, since they tend to be in the eyes of the beholder; then you deal with the fuzziness between A and not-A; then you figure that many As and Bs are not things that you can control; then you look around and notice that "all other things" have no intention of remaining equal. If you adhere too rigidly to that plan, you eventually walk away with a relic that fits the rules of method but yields limited truths about the human world that interested you in the first place.

Perhaps you take the map-making metaphor as a guide; for distance and elevation, precisely measured with transit and rod, you substitute human motion through space. Precisely measured by what? Transformed into what kind of representation? With what possible conclusions in mind? Even the comparatively simple symbolic world of a computer defies that approach. If you measure all the currents in all the circuits of the computer, would you know what it is doing?

Or perhaps you cling to your research identity but decide that the search for method is a blind alley. Instead you sneak up on the artists; they more than likely look on you as the whore at the garden party. But you argue to the researchers that you are still one of them; you use material from the humanscape in your statements, while the artist's work may contain nothing from the other side at all. The problem is that no one knows what you picked, how you picked it, and what you left behind. Why should a skeptic believe that what you say has anything to do with what the humanscape is like?

Humanscape exploration shares some characteristics of all of these approaches, but has intuition and serendipity added in. It is a method whose proper technical name is "ethnographic," roughly translatable as "folk-descriptive." When you explore humanscapes ethnographically, you bring back artifacts and experiences. One powerful humanscape artifact is the words of its occupants. So powerful are these artifacts that some explorers, like Oscar Lewis and Studs Terkel, simply sand and varnish them a bit and offer them directly to give a sense of the world in which their sayers live.

In addition to artifacts you bring back experiences, but they belong to you, the explorer. As you wander the territory and talk with its occupants, you *participate* in their activities and *observe* what is going on. Such experiences generate stories. Some of them you record; some of them you forget; some of them you don't need to record because you will never forget them. The experiences yield deep-seated understandings of some fundamental characteristics of the humanscape you are exploring. It is one thing to be told that the world is made out of Velveeta; it is another to walk around in it on a hot summer day.

The researcher aims for a statement that organizes artifacts and experiences to teach outsiders about a humanscape they have never seen (or perhaps seen so often that they have the illusion of knowing it). But the statements must rest on a method that contains two crucial ingredients. The first is an organization of the artifacts and experiences, a way of seeing them so that they reveal some truths about one humanscape to the occupants of another. The problem here is that the organization grows out of and changes with the relationship between artifacts, experiences, and explorer. The story of method for this research, for instance, is in part a story of organizational mistakes, mistakes that in turn reveal a better way to organize the material.

The second crucial ingredient is the principle of falsification, an essential part of the meaning of "research." The skeptic, unconvinced of the perfection of the explorer's insights, wonders what artifacts and experiences dropped out of sight, artifacts and experiences that might contain contradictions or other interesting complications. Not that researchers are liars, at least not any more so than the rest of humanity. But since what they offer is a way of seeing, one wonders just how much of the humanscape can in fact be seen that way.

The difficulty for humanscape explorers is that they return with truckloads of artifacts and experiences. Their problem is to work through this material in a way that both systematically organizes and potentially falsifies. To solve the problem, a strategy is borrowed from explorers of language, the strategy of setting the goal of accounting for a "corpus." The term refers—in linguistics—to a list of sentences that speakers have produced. The game is to use the corpus as an anchor for the development of rules to account for the organization of sound and meaning. The game is won when all the sentences are "accounted for."

The analogy gets complicated, because it is not clear what goes into the corpus when one leaves the neat world of the sentence. One solution is to pull out some portion of the total inventory of artifacts and experiences and declare them the corpus. It can serve as the material out of which you grow and against which you evaluate your understandings. You use other artifacts, your own experiences, your intuitions and creativity, and any other resources you can draw on, but you are "accountable" to the corpus—the pieces that fit and, most importantly as you go along, the pieces that do not.

That, in rough outline, is the ethnographic strategy for exploring humanscapes. In the research on independent truckers, the corpus is a series of interviews with independents about their careers in the trucking industry. The interviews and their analysis are more complicated than the usual precoded sociological survey. (Appendix I outlines the process.) In fact, such interviews, where the interviewee controls the topics and the way the talk unfolds, are some of the most notoriously difficult—but also most informative—raw material of social research. So time consuming is this kind of research that it limits the researcher to working with only a few people. So how, asks the statistically minded reader, do you know what you've got when you're done? How representative are your conclusions?

The Number Cruncher's Critique

The words of the independents are the artifacts, the material brought back from a world to give outsiders a sense of its texture. My own stories from trip experiences will supplement and modify them. By the end of the book, a reader should be as overwhelmed with pattern as I was working through the interviews. But still, the number-crunching skeptic's question remains. True, he or she will say, you don't need a large sample because you're looking at a world that any occupant must deal with and not at all the different kinds of occupants there are. And you've got a way to look systematically for pattern in a corpus that encourages falsification. Nevertheless, who's to say that kismet didn't throw you a curve?

There are several answers to that question. First, the career history interviews were obtained from a diverse group of independents. Second, the knowledge that is constructed in this study has been verified with independents around the country in truck stops, at loading and unloading points, at meetings, and at a course for independents sponsored by the Small Business Administration, one of a number held around the country in 1982. Third, other conclusions are items in letters, columns, and articles in *Owner-Operator, Overdrive, American Trucker*, and other independent trade magazines.

Even so, the number cruncher says. Fortunately, some surveys have already been done with independents, and those precrunched numbers can be coordinated with the exploration. Survey results are used to give evidence that the world learned about from a few is not just a peculiar statistical accident. The most important numbers come from the Interstate Commerce Commission (ICC) survey of independent truckers (ICC 1978, 1979). A third follow up in 1980 was not issued as a report, but the results are discussed in articles by Tom Corsi of the Business School at the University of Maryland, the researcher behind the survey. Its questions are the most methodologically sophisticated and well targeted. Other writings will be used as appropriate, particularly the work of Maister and Wyckoff. The numbers will add further support to the patterns in the corpus.

The Research Focus

This book focuses on a description of an occupational role in industrial and regulatory context, a description learned from a sample of those who bring that role to life. In the next chapter, the trucking industry is introduced and the sample members—the teachers—will begin speaking. Chapters 3 through 10 describe the different characteristics of their work by drawing from their own words on different topics that grew out of interviews, conversations, and observations. Chapter 11 pulls together the threads in the theme of "dependence" and contrasts it with two concepts of "independence," one representing the cultural ideal; the other, the current version that can realistically be achieved.

Missing, for the most part, are descriptions of the "Smokey and the Bandit" sort, the images developed in the popular literature discussed in detail in chapter 11. According to those images, an independent hangs around the truck stop, picks up an attractive young woman, tosses down a handful of pills, and takes off in his truck, playing country music and chattering on the CB as he goes.

On my trips, the only time we hung around a truck stop was when we could not get freight or the truck broke down; one of the most attractive young women I saw on my trips was a professional driver. No one that I traveled with took pills, although one does sometimes see glazed expressions. The person I worked with who most frequently played country music was Ike, the black independent introduced in the next chapter. Other preferences ran from silence to "easy listening" music. Although the CB radio was turned on during trips, its use by those I traveled with was usually instrumental—reports on "smokeys" (police), "chicken coops" (scale houses), "beavers" (women in "four-wheelers" or cars), and general road, traffic, and weather conditions.

Partying of course does go on; pills are available; unattached women show up at trucker social spots (a few of them also, in fact, truckers); country music is played; and some people get on the CB and chatter for hours. But to focus on that aspect of independent trucking, as much of the popular literature does, is to focus on one personal style (an atypical one, if my observations are representative) with little or no understanding of a complicated industry. The latter is what I was after, and the book's focus reflects that quest.

I also narrowed the focus by emphasizing the independent truckers' point of view. Trucking is a complicated industry involving a number of different professional roles in both the public and the private sectors. The company manager, the company driver, and the regulatory bureaucrat are not as well represented in this study as is the independent trucker. The goal here is to explore the nature of a role by learning about it from its occupants, not to describe all roles involved in trucking in equal detail.

Though the focus on independents should be kept in mind, material from corporate and regulatory sources is frequently drawn from throughout the book, as is literature either by or for regulatory decision makers, and material in the ICC archives. On a more personal level, I have benefited from helpful comments and advice from people interested in independent trucker issues from a variety of federal agency settings, as well as from my attendance at various hearings in those same agencies and in Congress. In fact, one contact led me to the Small Business Administration course for independent truckers. (Incidentally, I considered the course first rate, an opinion shared by almost all of the attendees I talked with.)

The company point of view is something I initially learned from my cited sources. My colleagues on the College of Business and Management's transportation faculty have also contributed to my education. After I completed the study, I presented a paper summarizing part of it to the national meetings of the Transportation Research Forum in late 1983. As a result of that presentation, I had several conversations with company managers that furthered my education.

Finally, the book narrows in on the working world of independents rather than attempting to describe everything they do. Obviously, such a focus leaves out other areas of life, like the family. At several points in the book, the wife appears as the business head in independent trucking. Several wives joked with me over the course of the research, insisting that I talk with them to find out what trucking is *really* all about. The joking was serious, and the general point was clear. Not only does the wife do the books; she often earns the second income that makes it possible to support the family. She also stays home, raises the children, turns down invitations to the neighborhood party because she does not want to go alone, and sometimes suffers neighborly suspicion about "what she does over there all the time" while he is gone.

Family life is not the only missing topic. What about the small but increasing number of women, working alone or in a team? (Since all my teachers, and most independents, are male I consistently use "he" in the text for indefinite third-person reference). What about the growing number of minorities? What about the "Convoy" generation, those who came in after the popular image developed, sometimes in direct response to it? Important topics all, but each of them will require at least as much research as did the work topic.

The goal of this book is to learn about an occupational role in its industrial context from those who play it in daily life. Next on the agenda is an introduction to this complicated industry, followed by a more personal introduction to the teachers without whom this book would not have been possible.

Chapter 2

Exploring
Trucking

The Trucking Industry

As a graduate student in anthropology I despaired of ever mastering the details of South Indian caste and kinship. The trucker's world makes the problem look simple by comparison. Once established, the trucking industry grew quickly, because only trucks provide quick door-to-door delivery of small shipments. Trucking facilitates inventory management and quick response to market changes in supply and demand. Trucks are the main "hardware" of American business.

It did not take long for the industry to get complicated. Trucking took off in the 1920s with the development of national highways and technologically sophisticated vehicles. In 1935, the Interstate Commerce Commission (ICC) drew trucking under its regulatory umbrella with the Motor Carrier Act. Although trucking was originally encouraged by the railroads as a local adjunct to their service, trucks quickly began to run away with the freight. Railroads were in large part responsible for moving the ICC (which had been regulating them since the late nineteenth century) over into trucking as well. The rivalry between the two modes of transport continues to this day.

The story of the interplay of politics, economics, and technology that led to the current situation in trucking would require another book. (Such histories are available—Karolevitz 1966, Russell 1971, Starr 1945, Thomas 1979.) The industry is now byzantine in its intricacy (see Fellmeth 1970 or Taff 1975, for recent but already outdated descriptions). Most important at the moment is the question of how *independents* fit in.

18   *Independents Declared*

It is a question that, until recently, few people knew enough to ask. The first oil embargo in 1973 engraved "independent truckers" in the national consciousness via the six o'clock news. Organizations proliferated, hearings were held, and popularizations abounded. The image was new, contrasting with the older stereotype of the Teamster driver of company-owned equipment, a stereotype that alternated between "knight of the road" and "thug." The presence of independents as a political force continues to the present, through two more shutdowns and several additional policy decisions. (Wyckoff and Maister, 1975, sketch the shutdown history and the growth of independent trucker organizations.)

Who are these independent truckers? A glance at any interstate highway reveals a variety of vehicles rolling by that are called "trucks," piloted by different kinds of people called "drivers." One type of truck is the *tractor-trailer*, so called because it has a *power unit*— the tractor, where the driver and the engine are—pulling a detachable trailer behind it. The trailer might be an ordinary van or *box*, or it might be a refrigerated trailer or *reefer*, or it might be a *flatbed*, or it might be a specialized trailer designed to pull heavy equipment, grain, or liquids. Then again, it might be a *bobtail*, a tractor driving along by itself with no trailer behind it (see Anderson's 1979 article on trailers.)

All tractors have a *steering* axle—the axle at the front. But some tractors have only one *drive* axle in the back, the axle where the engine power is delivered. Independents usually have tractors with two drive axles. Two axles, called *tandems* or *twin screws*, allow the truck to carry more weight. An independent's tractor usually has a large area behind the driver as well; in fact, it might be strikingly large. That is a *sleeper*, a place to sleep and store clothes, papers, and whatnot. It ranges in size from a small berth to a small room. *Company trucks* often have tandem drive axles and sleepers as well, but independents almost always have them because of the weight they carry, the length of the trips they take, and their greater need to save on motel bills.

Company trucks are owned by a variety of different companies or "carriers." One type of company runs its own trucks primarily to deliver its own goods. The driver of the truck is an employee of the same company. That type is called a *private* carrier. For example, Safeway has its own fleet of trucks to carry food from warehouses to stores; Levi-Strauss maintains a fleet to move its products from manufacturing centers to retail outlets. The ICC does not regulate private carriers; they are governed only by Department of Transportation (DOT) safety regulations.

Most of the trucks on the road are private carriers. One estimate holds that 57 percent of all interstate motor carriers are private (Eicher et al. 1982:II). Until recently, it was illegal for independents to work in private carriage, since they—not the company—own the truck and are not employees. In 1984 the ICC announced that independents could work for private carriers, but the decision was dragged into the courts by the next group—the *for-hire carriers*. So at the time of the study independents were not in private carriage—not legally, anyway.

For-hire carriers carry other people's freight. Everything that can be put on a truck is either *regulated* or *exempt*. Exempt freight tends to be closer-to-nature commodities such as unprocessed agricultural goods. Regulated freight tends to be things that have been touched by the human hand, or, more likely, by a machine. Most things that move by truck are regulated—manufactured goods, processed foods, and so on. If you're a *for-hire carrier*, and you're going to carry *regulated freight* across state lines, you've just entered into a meaningful relationship with the Interstate Commerce Commission.

There are many strands in the relationship, strands that are mutating in the current era of deregulation. But one of the most important of them is that the trucking company cannot just put anything it wants on its trucks and send them where the freight is in demand. The ICC regulates what the trucking company can carry as well as the places freight can be picked up and delivered.

Until recently this so-called *operating authority* was easier to get through merger than by application. If a carrier applied, other trucking companies having similar authority (not to mention railroads) protested. A protest led to lawyers, hearings, and more often than not, refusals of the application. In several trucking-company histories (Broehl 1954, Crouch 1975, Filgas 1967), carriers expanded primarily by buying other carriers that had the authority they wanted. But a new policy, "eased entry," has relaxed the old rules. In fact, legislation to drop economic regulation entirely is on the horizon.

The critical point for now is that one *cannot* get his hands on regulated freight without ICC authority. And by and large, independent truckers do not have it. (Reasons are discussed in chapter 4.) So an independent who wants to carry regulated freight across state lines has to *lease* himself and his truck to a carrier. The carrier provides the authority; the independent provides the truck and driver.

The ICC classifies for-hire carriers into a number of different types. Of significance here is that independents are not evenly distributed across all types. To oversimplify, there are traditionally two major patterns in for-hire trucking:

1) The carrier hauls general freight, which comes to it in bits and pieces. For this, it charges higher prices, or "rates," in part

because it has to maintain terminals to assemble and disassemble loads. It sends its tractor-trailers from one terminal to another; smaller trucks make the local deliveries after the tractor-trailers are unloaded. Carriers like these are the big boys of the industry—Consolidated Freightways, Pacific Intermountain Express, Roadway, and so on.

2) The carrier hauls "specialized commodities": things like household goods, building materials, refrigerated products, and heavy equipment. Specialized commodities tend to move in truckload quantities rather than in bits and pieces, so they are picked up at the shipper's and dropped at the customer's. Terminals are not necessary. Specialized commodity carriers move from region to region rather than from terminal to terminal. When the freight comes in truckload amounts, the rates are lower, and specialized commodities tend to be in the lower priced categories anyway.

There are exceptions to these patterns. But by and large leased independents work with the second kind of carrier—hauling truckloads of lower paying specialized commodities directly from shipper to customer.

In the last few years the carriers represented by the first pattern have started to use leased independents more and more. The way they do this is to set up a new office within the company called a "special commodities division" (Maister 1980). Maister discusses a study of sixty-four of these divisions, most of them established since 1965. Special commodities divisions are set up for the sole purpose of leasing independents to carry the same kind of freight sought by the carriers described in the second pattern. The "big boys" of the first pattern want the freight that the smaller carriers of the second pattern haul. The union (if present) tolerates the leased independents because the carrier could not afford to haul such freight using its own trucks and employed drivers.

Whatever carrier they are leased to, though, independents cluster in the low-paying freight niches of trucking. But in those niches they perform much of the work, with their share on the rise since 1965. Overall, independents account for about 25 percent of the interstate miles traveled by regulated carriers (Maister 1980:10). In this area of the trucking industry are most of the independents— leased on to regulated, for-hire carriers.

A substantial minority of independent truckers also haul exempt freight. When the ICC moved into trucking in the 1930s, agricultural interests prevented regulation of farm trucks. If a truck hauls exempt commodities, primarily unprocessed agricultural goods, the ICC is not involved. A driver in his own truck who primarily hauls exempt commodities is an independent by definition. People in the industry consider this style of independence "the real thing." But the focus in this book is on the leased independent. Most truckers who own and operate their own tractor work through a lease.

A last complication. Whatever their primary style, independents typically mix leased and exempt trips. So for example, an independent leased to a carrier might haul regulated freight from the Northeast out to the West Coast, but then return with an exempt load of fresh fruit. Or an independent who primarily hauls exempt freight might find himself in Chicago, where he takes on a load of regulated freight for just a single trip to get back to Florida. Even though such mixtures are the norm, an independent will readily place himself as either a "leased" or an "exempt" hauler.

Some independents "haul exempt." A few now (1986) experiment with new opportunities in private carriage. (Incidentally, one reason why the for-hire carriers took the decision to court is apparent; they stand to lose their captive audience.) But most independents cluster among the for-hire carriers, especially in the lower rated specialized commodity area.

How many independents are there? Wyckoff and Maister (1975) estimated 100,000 in the mid-1970s. Maister (1980) quotes a report estimating the "number of truckers who consider themselves self-employed, reported more than $400 in net earnings and have not reached the taxable maximum for social security purposes" as about 130,000 in 1974. The ICC estimated about 61,000 were used among the larger regulated carriers. No one knows for sure, but 100,000 is a good working number.

This book deals only with one kind of independent trucker, the kind who leases himself and his truck to a for-hire carrier. The Small Business Administration finds that 75 percent of independents work in this way. Wyckoff (1979:85) estimates 67 percent; Eicher and co-authors estimate about 60 percent (1982:vi). From these statistics and my own impressions talking to drivers on cross-country trips, it is clear that most independents are leased, although many drivers hop around, not only from regulated to exempt and back, but from independent to company employee and the reverse. But for now, a circle has been drawn around the territory to be explored. The problem is that some technical ambiguities in the term "independent" remain.

Independence Defined

The "independent" in "leased independent" is a slippery term. When independents work in the for-hire segment of trucking, they do so in part because it is the traditional way they can haul regulated freight. They are not really independent, although they are independent contractors.

Sort of. There is a continuing debate—is the leased independent trucker in fact an employee or a contractor? Wyckoff and Maister review the issue in their earlier book, and Maister updates to 1980. The argument involves the National Labor Relations Board, the Internal Revenue Service, the worker's compensation boards of different states, and the Teamsters, not to mention independents and carriers. Maister (1980:148) presents the checklist used to determine, more or less, whether one is an employee or a contractor. Most of the independents I know do consider themselves small businessmen that contract out their services.

Though I use "independent" for someone who is leased to a carrier, the more correct technical term (for both leased and exempt) is "owner/operator"—a person who owns and operates one or more trucks without ICC authority. (Corsi, 1979, writes that 66 percent of his sample of owner/operators had one truck, 18 percent had two to five trucks, the rest, even more.) Some say that the only "real" independents are the owner/operators who primarily haul exempt freight. Those who lease to carriers are somehow blemished by comparison. The blemishes fade a bit when you realize that exempt haulers work through brokers and deal with different state jurisdictions too.

One last item of terminological confusion. Owner/operators may drive vehicles other than tractor-trailers, and they do not necessarily drive from state to state. I spent an interesting evening speaking with a couple in Virginia who each drove a "ten-wheeler" dump truck, only within the state; they owned and operated the vehicles, and many of their opinions were not very different from those of independents who drive interstate. In a small Maryland town near the Pennsylvania border, an independent pointed out the school buses parked in a yard; they were owned and operated by town residents and leased to the school system. In the Sierra Nevada foothills in California I interviewed an owner/operator who worked only intrastate, hauling lumber down to southern California and building materials back to the north.

"Independent" is not a particularly crisp concept. In this study, I am concerned with only one variation on the many themes that it includes—leased owner/operators who own and drive a tractor-trailer combination over interstate routes. Statistically, that type of owner/operator is the most common type of interstate independent trucker and is the kind of trucker I mean when I use the term "independent," in the sense of "independent contractor." Truckers refer to themselves as independents too, though, more often, "owner/operators," and less frequently "contractors" and "brokers." But seldom do they "gypsy," hauling mostly exempt loads, or run as "outlaws," carrying freight in violation of the rules of the ICC game.

The World of Trucking

So far, independent trucking has been discussed generally as a role in an industry with a peculiar regulatory and economic history. The actual independent trucker humanscape still has not been approached. Exploration of that humanscape requires good guides, teachers who can show a stranger around and describe what is going on. People, the truism goes, live in worlds endowed with meaning, embedded in webs of significance, littered with definitions of the situation, aglow with constituted realities. To understand the texture of a world requires some teaching from its occupants. Distant observation simply does not lead to much understanding.

The researcher has several ways to pick teachers. One way is to take everyone who dwells in a humanscape and randomly draw a sample of a hundred occupants. The researcher talks to each one just long enough to answer a short list of questions he made up. Then he statistically analyzes the pattern of answers. That model of humanscape exploration has its place, but it is no way to pick a teacher.

A better model is based on a choice of occupants of a humanscape with whom the researcher's relationships are good and who are willing to take him on as a student. Rather than a short list of standardized questions, he has several conversations, some of them in the midst of tasks that are the activities of which the occupants' world is made. The researcher works with more than one teacher to prevent locking onto one idiosyncratic style, but the emphasis is on quality of understanding that comes from contact with a few good teachers rather than quantity of people contacted.

My teachers mostly came from the Maryland Independent Truckers and Drivers Association. When I first considered this work I had just moved to the University of Maryland. Tom Corsi of the University of Maryland Business School introduced me to some of the ICC staff concerned with independents, and they in turn led me to Rita Bontz. In the fall of 1981 Rita was not affiliated with MITDA; she is currently the president, and has made the organization into an effective regional independent trade association. She sent me to the next meeting of the organization. I was invited to describe my research, did so, and was treated to my first lesson in the contradiction between independence and control as the independents discussed the popularization of their profession.

I have been participating in the organization ever since, attending monthly meetings and social events, and most recently working as secretary and helping design a survey to document problems with freight rates. When possible I also attend hearings and meetings at which MITDA representatives present testimony. A more dedicated group of teachers is hard to imagine. If I did not get it right, it is not their fault. If I did, it is mostly thanks to their patient teaching of an interested outsider.

In addition to hundreds of conversations with MITDA members and other independent truckers at local truckstops and on long-distance trips, seventeen independents (ten of them MITDA members) were interviewed on tape about their "career history." This book is built on a corpus consisting of ten of those interviews. (Two of the ten were interviewed at the same time.)

Seven were chosen for the corpus because they were done with independents with whom I had traveled. I spent about forty "road-days"—days actually moving or involved in the details of a trip. Three trips were long distance; one from Baltimore to Portland via North Dakota and then back to Baltimore after a drop in New York City; the second from Baltimore to New York, then to Dallas and Houston and the Texas Valley and back to Baltimore; the third from Baltimore to Gary, Indiana, and back. There were also three daytrips in the northeast corridor; one to Newark and back; one to Philadelphia and back; and one doing local work in the Baltimore area.

After including those seven interviews, I rejected a different seven. Three were done with intra- rather than interstate truckers; one interview was with a driver who worked for a company but owned another truck and employed its driver; another interviewee had spent only a few years as an independent and then quit; one interview was not transcribed, and in another my tape recorder failed. Of course, I learned much from these interviews as well.

Three more interviews were then added to the corpus to make a total of nine interviews with ten people. One was with an independent recently retired; another with one recently turned dispatcher; but both had been in the business most of their working lives. The third was a younger independent who dropped in during the dispatcher's interview, stayed, got interested, and became part of the research.

The career history interviews are the corpus, the anchor for the exploration of the independent trucker humanscape. The many other conversations, meetings and social events, the hours in the ICC archives, the interstate trips—all are resources to draw from in the work of accounting for the humanscape. To understand the interview content it is necessary to know something about the primary teachers.

The Teachers

The teachers who showed me independent trucking are a varied lot. I met Red first. When I moved to the University of Maryland in August 1981, I was introduced to some regulators at the ICC, the first of many federal bureaucrats with an interest in independent trucking who gave generously of their time and advice. (The others included congressional staff members and employees of the Department of Transportation and the Small Business Administration.) An ICC colleague, in turn, was my contact with Rita Bontz, wife of an independent trucker, and an activist in "trucker politics."

My research fit in with her agenda of educating the public on the realities of independent trucking. She welcomed me into her home, almost drowned me in material from her files, and told me she would try to line up an interview or two. A short time later she telephoned and said I should meet Red, who was in town for a couple of days. Could I come up? I could and did. We drove a couple of miles to a paved lot next to a diesel engine sales and repair shop, a place where Red was allowed to park his tractor when he was in town. Since it was Sunday, the lot was empty. But in the back sat a tractor being attended to by my first teacher.

Red was changing a tire. He greeted me, took a can of soda from Rita, who then left to do some errands, and started explaining the difference between Budd and Dayton wheels. He interrupted himself, said, "Rita says you're interested in something called participant observation, that right?" I nodded. "Well then, grab that wrench and hold this thing, will you?" So began my education.

Red is the only college-educated teacher. Some of my teachers never finished high school, but Red has a bachelor's degree in agriculture. He started trucking late in life, at age thirty-six in 1964, but he began as an independent. Now, at age fifty-six, he is divorced from his second wife, and has two children from his first marriage. The oldest of four half-siblings, he currently lives in his own home in Baltimore when he is not on the road. We did the interview during a trip from Baltimore to Portland, Oregon, in January of 1982. I still see Red at meetings, at social events, and occasionally in Washington at hearings.

Jack's interview appears second in the next section of this chapter. Shortly after the first Baltimore meeting I attended in October

1981, Jack invited me to his house to show me the paperwork involved in a trip. He lives in his own home in the Baltimore area with his wife and the youngest of his five children, who was still at home recovering from a motorcycle accident at the time. Jack, who is now forty-eight years old, is the youngest of six children. His father and a brother worked for the "enemy" railroad, as he put it. He began work as a company driver in 1959, moving to independent status more recently in 1974. We did the interview in his living room after a family dinner of crab soup, and some months later, in June of 1982, I went on a trip with him to Chicago. I saw Jack regularly until recently, when he left the organization because of a disagreement over the group's position on the January 1983 independent truckers' shutdown.

Steve, the third quoted teacher, heard about my research and called with a request to be interviewed. At age fifty-eight, he has been in the business since 1949. A confirmed bachelor with one older sibling, he lives in his own home in the Baltimore area. A few years ago Steve left the road to become the local dispatcher for a midwestern trucking company. When I arrived in his Baltimore office to interview him, he had gathered a collection of history books, old photographs, and industry publications to lend to me. His interview, the first one I conducted, was also the longest.

Toward the latter part of the interview, a younger independent, about thirty years old, came in to pick up his paperwork, got involved in what we were doing, and became part of the interview. Dave is single, a West Virginian who, after a few years as a leased owner/operator, decided to become a "gypsy"—picking up exempt loads and trip-leasing. After the interview I had no contact with Dave, except by exchanging greetings occasionally through Steve.

Cal, at sixty-four the oldest teacher, is from a trucking family, with a father, a brother, and a son who also work in the industry. He lives in his own home just over the Maryland line in Pennsylvania with his second wife. Cal is the oldest of six siblings, and is currently retired because of illness. Until recently, though, he worked as an independent, something he has done almost continuously since his entry into trucking in 1945.

We did the interview in his dining room, with his wife present for most of it. She explained that she enjoys hearing Cal talk about trucking and wanted to listen, though she also frequently attended to the television in the corner. Cal's style turned more formal than usual during the taping, compared to the many conversations about trucking that we had before the interview and that we have had since. Afterward he gave me a tour of his shop in the large garage next to his house. Cal's interview shows that he is one of the most mechanically sophisticated owner/operators around.

I met Dan in Nevada when Red's tractor broke down, a story related later in this study. Dan and his wife recently got their own ICC authority, but are unhappy with it for reasons described later. He had just purchased a new tractor and flatbed trailer for about a hundred thousand dollars. When Red's truck broke down, the tow-truck operator introduced us, and Red and Dan agreed that we would put Dan's tractor under Red's trailer so we could get the perishable load of produce delivered to New York.

Dan is the oldest of four siblings, currently living with his wife and three children in his own home. Now forty years old, he began driving off-highway at age fifteen. He bought his first truck in 1973 and now runs a fleet of three, counting the new one. Over the several days we were in Nevada, he and his family were extremely hospitable, providing laundry facilities and a feast before we headed east. His wife also gave me an education in the process of applying for state permits. We did the interview on the trip to New York. Afterward, Dan mentioned his surprise at the easiness of the interview and at his own openness.

Will is the independent I have had least contact with, both before and after the interview. But occasionally in research, as in life, you run into someone who just speaks the same language. We met at a meeting, talked, and when I explained my work and asked for an interview Will agreed with great interest. We did the interview in the kitchen of the house he owns in rural Maryland. His wife and two daughters left us to run errands. With a coffee pot brewing in the background, we began the interview.

Will, now forty-eight years old, began his trucking career in 1952 at the age of eighteen, becoming an independent in 1979. He is the oldest of nine brothers and sisters. Trucking runs in his family: Will's father drove a truck and used to take him along on some local deliveries. Will's interview style is no different from his conversational style.

Irv is, with Carl, the most active organization member among the teachers. At sixty years of age, he recently got tired of long hauls and now pulls containers from the Baltimore port around the region. I accompanied him on one trip from Baltimore to Philadelphia and back, during which we did the interview. Irv paid me the compliment of saying that he enjoyed the interview and conversation so much that it was the first time he had not turned on his CB all day. We still talk frequently, and invariably he has a good idea for some kind of study.

Married with five children, Irv lives in his own home in the

Independents Declared

Baltimore area. He began driving in about 1945 as a company driver, moving quickly into partnership to buy his own truck in 1946. He is the youngest child with two older sisters. Trucking is also in his family, as he had uncles who drove and his son is also an independent.

Carl was the Baltimore organization member who was asked to look out for me at the first meeting I attended in October 1981. He began driving a company truck in about 1940 at age seventeen. By 1948, he had purchased his own truck and became an independent. The youngest of three, he is married with three children, and currently lives in his own home in Baltimore. Recently he experienced one of those inevitable mechanical disasters when his tractor engine blew up. Now, at age fifty-eight, he has purchased an older tractor and works in the region, picking up a loaded trailer at a terminal and making several drops in the area. The day I spent working with him was also the day I interviewed him, partly in a fast-food restaurant and partly in the truck. By comparison with our usual conversations, Carl's interview was somewhat formal, though he relaxed toward the end. I still see him regularly at meetings and social events.

Ike, the only black teacher, is among the younger of thirteen siblings, six of whom died in childhood. Raised in rural North Carolina, he began driving at age fifteen in 1942. Now fifty-four years old, he lives in his own home with his wife and two children in the Baltimore area. He became an independent in 1966, and since that time has owned more than one truck and recently got his own ICC authority.

Ike is, by his own account, a man of action rather than words. For that reason, it is no surprise that his interest in my work led him to invite me on a trip where I could be shown rather than told. I took the trip to Texas and back, and during it we did the interview. For the same reason, it should be no surprise that Ike's interview is the briefest. Ike also taught me, through the stories he told and the places he showed me, that a study should be done of black (and other minority) experiences in trucking. In this study, though, the focus is on the world the teachers share rather than the differences among them.

The teachers are experienced participants in the trucking industry and have different mixtures of company and independent trucking work histories. Most are people I knew before the official interview, and most are people I still see regularly at organization meetings and social events. All are articulate and offer rich descriptions of the world in which they work. All share with many other independents a theory that outsiders have little sense of the details of their work and a desire to remedy that problem. That is at least part of the reason why they took me on as a student of their working world. Our agendas overlapped when I approached them to help me do this study.

Getting into Trucking

Now the teachers may begin to speak for themselves. They start by telling how they got into the trucking business.

The following conventions are used for quotes. Because I did not do detailed linguistic analyses, verbatim transcription was not necessary, and some minimal editing made the passages more readable. My words (in parentheses) were left in if they were part of the independent's change of direction or elaboration on a topic. A word or phrase in brackets explains some detail. An ellipsis (". . .") indicates an unintelligible portion of the transcript. Names of both people and carriers are pseudonyms.

The first story best fits the romantic image of becoming an independent trucker. Following is Red's account of how he got into trucking:

> Ever since I was a little kid I've always been attracted to trucks, I guess, machinery of all sorts. When I was in grade school even, we used to go up on the main road, which was right close to my house, and watch the trucks go by, and waved at the drivers. And then after a while we developed a game where we were trying to guess what kind of a truck was coming by—well, like after dark, just by the sound of it. And later on when I started working weekends and during summer vacation I went to work at my grandfather's builders' supply yard. Even before I had a driver's license I used to drive the trucks around the yard off the street, filling orders, loading the trucks. And that was the biggest thrill in the world, was whenever I got to drive the truck around a little bit. So I made up my mind pretty early that I would kind of like to be a trucker.
>
> So when it came that fateful time when I was about ready to finish high school and my dad asked me what I wanted to do with my life, I told him I wanted to be a truck driver. He just totally ignored that. Never even commented. He said, "Well, what do you think about going up to state college and learning scientific agriculture?" Well, due to a chain of circumstances I never really got into agriculture, but I worked at a couple different things over the years. And the last job I had before I started trucking I was a salesman. It got to be an everyday thing when I'd be driving down the road from home, going to my territory, I'd see these trucks going down the Beltway, down through the Harbor Tunnel and all. And I—jees, you know, if I could only go with them, just tag along behind them and go wherever they're going instead of going down here and calling on these druggists and doctors and all that junk. So I just got progressively more and more unhappy with my sales work.

Independents Declared

And one day—I guess I was about thirty-six—and I just thought, jees, you know, am I going to be spending the rest of my life doing something that I really actually hate doing? And the answer of course was no. So I did a lot of finagling around. I borrowed some money, and I saved every penny I could, and I finally went out—well, I shopped around. First I tried to buy a new truck, and it was too much money. I couldn't get anybody to finance one for me because of no experience or anything. So finally I did get a credit approval for a five-year-old tractor that was just about worn out when I got it.

Red goes on to describe the truck, the resistance of his wife to his decision, and his first job.

The story provides a good fit with many nontruckers' images of what such a story should be like. It describes a triumphant personal struggle to achieve a romantic identity—independent trucker—even at the cost of social approval. The process of achieving it mirrors in many ways the characteristic it is supposed to represent—independence. Interestingly enough, this story is told by the one teacher with a college degree and a white-collar job who entered trucking comparatively late in life.

A different sort of story comes from Jack, an independent without a high school diploma who began trucking in his early twenties. Jack was working as a "cooker" at a distillery when he got sick for a couple of days. Because of some aspect of the company's health plan, it made sense for him to stay home the entire week. So when a friend asked if he wanted to work with him, Jack accepted the invitation:

So I had a buddy who was driving for ABC Motor Freight. And he said to me, "Jack," he said, "come on you want to ride with me?" I was in my twenties then. So I says, "Yeah." I says, "Hell, I ain't doing nothing." I always wanted to do it anyway, you know. So we went and asked the terminal manager. [story about the old days omitted] So we get back to the terminal Friday and Don called me in the office, and he asked me if I wanted a job. And I asked him, doing what? He said driving a truck, a truck driver. I turned around and told him, I said, "Oh hell." I said, "Yeah, I'd love to have a goddamn job like this," you know. I said, "Man, it's something I always wanted to do. I dreamt of doing this, you know, but I never had the opportunity to do it. And nobody'd give me a break to do it. And now I can't do it because I got all these children."

Then he said, "Well," he said, "I'll tell you what I'll do." I still don't know how to drive a truck that good, you know. I couldn't back a truck up at all. I didn't know how to back one up. He said, "Well, I'll tell you what I'll turn around and do." See, I was helping my buddy jockey the trucks in the evening, you know, backing them in up against the platforms and stuff. And I was getting a little expe-

rience that way. But I wasn't getting paid for it, see. And he seen me.
I was trying to learn it you know, and the man seen I was trying to
learn. So he offered me the job.

He says, "I'll give you Casey, the old colored fellow out on the
platform." He said, "I'll give you Casey for one week as a helper."
He says, "If you don't bring that truck back in pieces, no crumpled
fenders or anything like that, in a week, I'll put you on." He says,
"I'll write a letter to the union hall asking them to accept you as a
Teamster." Then he said, "I'll put you on payroll down here as a city
man." He said, "But I'm only giving you Casey for one week, and if
you can't learn in one week you ain't going to be a truck driver."
And he says, "That's the conditions I'll give him to you." And I says,
"You mean it? You're honest about it?" I says, "Yeah I'll take the
gamble. I'll gamble it." And he says, "O.K., you're hired."

Red and Jack both reflect a favorable view of trucking; both show
the relationship between narrator and occupation to be positive. But
the descriptions of the path to the occupation differ dramatically.
Red, the college-educated white-collar worker, describes his path in
terms of free choice and personal effort. Jack, the less well-educated
laborer, tells it as "lucking into" a situation in which he does work
for which he asks nothing, followed by astonishment when he is
offered the job. Both Red and Jack get what they want, but their
descriptions differ in ways that an analysis in terms of class would
predict. And unlike Red, Jack does not start out as an independent;
he goes to work as a Teamster company driver.

Steve, like Jack, was introduced to trucking by chance:

Back during World War II when I took my army physical I was
turned down. And to try to get it fixed up so I could get in the service I had an operation in 1944, which in my estimation had reper-
cussions in 1946 and '47. I started to suffer with headaches. Well, I
had them for eleven months straight, at least a week out of every
month and one month there I had them every day. Consequently I
was unable to keep a job for very long because of absenteeism. And
in looking for work I ended up driving a dump truck over at Spar-
rows Point, the steel mill. It was midsummer. I never could take
heat very good. It was dusty, and with the heat I figured I'd last
maybe about three days. But when I went to working outside my
headache stopped. I was doing construction work and was doing O.K.
as far as the headaches, but construction back in the late '40s, you
worked all summer and then starved to death all winter.

Well, it so happened that some people that I was dealing with on
tires for my car had connections with ABC Truck Lines as one of
their contacts on truck tires. And they said that they could get me a
job driving with ABC, buying my own truck. And in order to stay
working outside and working year around I bought my first truck in

1949 through this connection with the tire company here. And that's how I started trucking.

Steve describes an illness that limits the jobs he can do. Trucking is the solution, allowing him to work all year and still remain outside. Instead of winding up in trucking as one possibility among several, like Red, trucking is the *only* possibility. The story differs from Jack's in that Steve does not describe trucking as a valued occupation. Cal's story, also involving illness, shows similarities to Steve's:

I tried a lot of things. I was an automobile mechanic, and I had a lot of trouble with this disease for years. See, I had a lot of operations starting when I was twelve years old. And this is what it does to you. [shows scars] That and I have a artificial elbow, and you apply for a good job and the first thing is the examination. That's it. I tried to get in Bethlehem Steel for years. I couldn't get in there. I couldn't get no place a good job. That's what put me to driving truck, because, well, I was getting older, and I just wanted to try to get ahead a little bit, that's all.

Like Steve, Cal has a physical problem that limits the possible jobs he can do. Cal also puts a comparatively low value on trucking in this passage, contrasting it twice with a "good" job. But there is more of a sense of personal choice here; Cal chose trucking because he wanted to get ahead.

So far, several variations among the stories have been identified: whether or not trucking is a desirable occupation; whether or not trucking is the only possible choice; whether or not the individual worked to bring it about; and whether or not he began as an independent, owning and operating his own truck. Irv's story adds yet another variation; the opportunity came up by chance and he grabbed it:

Well, how I got into trucking. Let me see. I was driving a taxicab. I guess I'd probably been married about six months or something like that. And I was out with a friend of mine one night. We was in a bar up on Charles Street having a beer. And he looked at his watch. He said, "Holy smokes, I got to call in." I says, "For what?" He said, "Go to work." Said, "What do you mean go to work? This's night time." He said, "Well, you want to make some money?" I said, "What kind of money?" He said, "Well, go to New York." I said, "I ain't lost nothing in New York." He said, "It pays you $16.40." I said, "What are you waiting for?"

So he was pulling for Transfer and Storage, called them up. They told him he had a trip to New York. He said, "You need any extra drivers?" This is during World War II. He said, "Do you need any extra drivers?" He [the dispatcher] said, "This guy have a license?" He said, "Yeah." Said, "social security card?" He said, "Yeah." He said, "Bring him in with you. Don't let him get away." In other words they was hurting for drivers. They didn't care whether you knew how to drive a truck or not, as long as you had a license and social security card.

So we went in, and they give me a old K8 International, and my buddy was driving a WA 22 White. Now believe it or not this is the second time I ever been in a truck. The first time I got in one as a passenger and rode from Baltimore to Edgewood and back. I'm talking about trucks as we know them today. 'Course they were gasoline engine trucks. They wasn't as big as they are now but they had improved quite a bit since I'd been with my uncle. I was only like six years old when I rode with him.

So he takes me over there. We get in these trucks and we start up the road. And he told me what the shift pattern was. A five-speed transmission. That's all you got. So we start up the road. To make a long story short, it took me twelve hours to drive from Baltimore to New York. So, in other words, I learned to drive a truck on my own. Nobody taught me anything. They just said, there it is, take off.

From taxis to trucks, mainly through a chance contact and motivation to follow through because of the money. Unlike the others (except perhaps Red), Irv had a previous job as a driver. And, like Red, he emphasizes his lack of training. He jumps into the truck and figures it out from there. Carl also moved from a previous driving job into trucking:

I was driving a bus for a hotel in Jersey, Wildwood, New Jersey. It was only a summer job. I was probably about seventeen. I met a fellow and a girl out there, and he was driving for a produce company, a straight job [single-unit truck]. So he said, "When the bus season's over I can get you on driving a straight job hauling produce around the Jersey shore." So I did that for a while. Didn't particularly like it. Then I heard that some milk truck company from Pennsylvania had a Jersey run—Cape May, Wildwood, Atlantic City—delivering milk. So we went to West Chester, Pennsylvania, and signed on. And that's what I run for about a year—Wildwood-Atlantic City-Cape May.

Carl changes from a bus to a "straight job" (truck where the power unit and cargo area are mounted on the same chassis) to a tractor-trailer, all because of a chance contact.

Other stories also show continuity in the driving role. As a teenager Dan works for a friend of the family hauling equipment off-highway; when he is old enough he gets his license and begins his over-the-road career. Will works in a meat-packing house, where he sometimes travels with drivers to help unload. He had also ridden with his father and later drove a straight job making deliveries for a hardware manufacturer. One day the dispatcher needed a driver urgently and Will volunteered, figuring out how to drive the tractor-trailer as he took off down U.S. Route 1.

Ike's account is the last story of entering trucking:

Well, when I first started driving a truck I started back in 19 and 41, 42. I was fifteen years old. I worked on a farm and at the end of the year—about a year working at a sawmill—got a job making thirteen dollars a week. I was hauling logs out of a sawmill, out of the woods from the sawmill to the planing mill. And one day the old man carried me into town. He wanted to go in there and get some feed for the horse and carried me down back to the courthouse. And I asked him what was he going to do, put me in jail? And he told me, "No, we're going down here and get a piece of paper." I didn't know what kind of paper he was talking about.

Goes on down there, and a big old man was sitting there, and there was Murdock. Weighed about five hundred pound. Captain said, "What do you bring that boy down here for?" . . . Said, "I want to get him his license." He said, "How old is he?" He said, "He's fifteen, soon be sixteen, but I need him." He gave me a set of license.

I started hauling lumber from the mill out of the woods to the planing mill and one day the driver didn't show up. He told me he wanted me to—asked me could I drive that truck there to Petersburg. I told him, "Yeah, I try." Loaded it down with green lumber from Greenville, North Carolina. I went into Petersburg, dropped the load off. Called the next morning and next day after I got unloaded he told me, "Come on back." I get back, he had another trailer sitting there and he told me, "Well, you might as well take that one on back. Romey ain't showed up." I carried that one on back up there and had a heck of a time trying to back it in. Old pole trailer [trailer with its own front axle, attached to tractor by a boom or "pole"].

So I got back and he said, "Alright." Romey came in. He said, "Well, since you're doing such a good job"—he went in town and he bought him a brand new Chevrolet. He gave that one to Romey and told me to keep the old one and I went into Washington, D.C. Left out of Washington, went up to Philadelphia, came back down.

Ike, a black man in rural North Carolina, tells his story with no description of the desirability of trucking or his personal role. He does what his white boss tells him to do in the story world of the early 1940s.

The stories provide a lesson in variability. In the ideal story of independence the interviewee should describe trucking as a positively valued career, and how he chose it for positive reasons, not because it was the only possible choice under the circumstances. He should describe how he started as an independent right at the beginning. And to really emphasize the independence image, he should say something about overcoming a lack of training and breaking courageously with an undesirable prior job involving supervision and control.

Red's is the ideal story. The others depart from the ideal more or less. Particularly striking is the number who do not particularly idealize trucking, who describe their entry in terms of fortuitous circumstances, and who did not begin as independents. Finally, it is ironic that the two who vary most from the ideal—Dan and Ike—are the two who recently obtained their own operating authority under the 1980 regulatory reforms.

These nine independent truckers (plus the one who dropped in to Steve's interview, not described here) gave the career history interviews that make up the corpus of this study. As previously related, their ages range from early forties to mid-sixties. With the exception of Red, the highest educational level is high school—some did not get that far—and most have worked in trucking since early adulthood, if not before. With the exception of Red and Steve, they have families with working wives. Some live in the city; some in the country. All live in their own homes. During the recession ongoing at the time of this research none of them made much profit trucking.

Originally, I planned to include in this study some detailed economic material. But I soon learned that these men would be easily identified by their friends. Because of this, and because of their understandable sensitivity about having their books put out on the street for everybody to see, I use aggregate economic data from the surveys instead. The main conclusion from informal conversations was that independent trucking was not good business during the research period. In many cases, if it were not for the wife's income, the truck would be gone. No one was getting rich. The best figures I heard were fifteen to twenty thousand dollars a year net profit. The worst was a very few thousand dollars. The ICC study showed that among independents who were still leased to the same carrier one year after the original survey, 34 percent reported earning less than ten thousand dollars before taxes; 48 percent earned between ten and twenty thousand. These figures are for 1977, and among those who were out of trucking or among those who had leased on with a new carrier a year later, the percentages earning under ten thousand dollars jumped to 70 percent and 66 percent, respectively (ICC 1979:83-85).

Independent costs are difficult to pin down, especially when the business and household budgets blur together, and when records are sometimes kept on the back of an old envelope. One general figure, based on a survey reported in the industry weekly *Transport Topics* (March 25, 1985) lists these cost estimates: Fees and licenses, $7,199.53; insurance, $4,400.00; fuel, $22,680.00; truck payments/repairs,

$15,600.00; prorated engine overhaul, $1,142.00; maintenance, $4,008.00; motels, $602.00; food, $4,489.00; unpaid miles, $3,184.00; return on investment, $2,500.00; miscellaneous, $1,000.00; salary (including benefits and before federal, state, and local income tax), $38,548.00. These figures were developed by a company that finances independents' tractor purchases.

The grand total is $105,352.53. Sometimes you hear people outside the industry say that a trucker told them he "made" a hundred thousand dollars in a year. What the outsider misunderstands is that the figure is the gross revenue before costs are deducted. For the hypothetical independent described in the survey, one hundred thousand dollars a year leaves him five thousand short of his goal.

Other economic details are mentioned throughout the interviews. For now, the wealth of information in the career history interviews is available to show how independents view their work. Since the teachers are older and experienced (as teachers should be), they told several stories about the "old days." Such stories are a good place to begin, since they explain leasing and how it came about.

Chapter 3

The
Old Days

The Road Life

The point of a "career history" interview is not really history; it is just a convenient format through which independent truckers express their perspectives on trucking. But you cannot talk to experienced independents without learning something about their image of the "good old days." One particular angle on the old days led me to some truths about the history of ICC policy that goes a long way toward explaining the rationale of leases. Other historical material ranged over a variety of topics. Occasionally a story about someone even went all the way back to pre-ICC trucking, since pre-ICC was only fifty years ago. But for the most part, the trucking memories among the older interviewees start at about World War II.

In some ways they sound like anyone talking about thirty or forty years ago—lower prices, simpler times, less complicated lives. Occasionally they make comments that summarize some of the changes in trucking one would expect to hear about—more sophisticated trucks, improved roads, and the appearance of franchised truck stops. Steve, for example, reminisced about trucks:

> Of course, the trucks are better because the horsepower's higher. You hardly ever see anybody without a sleeper anymore. In fact, when I started, everybody was sleeping across the seat or leaning against the door. Very few sleepers then. (That must have been uncomfortable.) When you're six-foot-four. 'Course there was a lot of gas trucks then, and I don't know about the other guys, but I was afraid in the cool weather to run the heater because of asphyxiation.
>
> With the diesel there isn't that risk. The funny thing about it, the owner/operator was probably the first to go—now I'm talking this

part of the country. The West has had diesels for years. The West and the Rockies have been like the pioneers of trucking, I guess mostly because of the terrain. I mean, you've got the Rockies. You've got the Sierras. The Cascades in the Northwest. You've got all that mountainous country plus you got all those logging companies out there. They just couldn't get by with the kind of equipment we use back here. Mostly terrain, I would say.

And, of course, their laws were a lot more lenient out there. They could afford to be more lenient, because you could figure most of the cities out that way were, say, a hundred years newer. You take like Boston. A lot of that stuff was probably there when Paul Revere was trying to get that horse around. Now that horse no doubt would go places today's trucks would not go. But the streets are still there like that. And naturally the lengths were much shorter back here. Lot of restrictions.

I don't know whether they still do it or not out on the West Coast—I don't think they do—but years ago they used to have extremely long tractors out there with not too long a trailer. It was just because the way the law was set up out there. You had to have this extreme length from the steering axle to your trailer axle, and you would find tractors with wheelbases of two hundred and some to three hundred and some inches out there. You figure an ordinary wheelbase around here back in the '40s was like 140-some inches. Well, I had a tractor that was actually set up for the West with a single axle. It had a 188-inch wheelbase for a single axle. I can show you tandems [tractor with two drive axles] that don't even run that long a wheelbase.

Steve's comments center on the development of the tractor in the direction of greater comfort and power, arguing that trucks developed more quickly in the West because of newer roads, more rugged mountains, and a more lenient regulatory environment.

Carl told a story about an early cross-country trip, before interstates, in a "gas job," a truck with a gasoline engine. He concluded that "when I was out there (in California) I tried to sell it. I was going to come home on a bus." One does not have to go much farther back than Carl and Steve to find the pioneers of trucking, rattling their bones at fifteen miles per hour on solid rubber tires, sitting in exposed cabs, and slamming into ruts or sinking in mud on unimproved roads. As far as trucks go, today's trucker, in his air-conditioned cab with an air-ride seat, is much better off.

Facilities on the side of the road have also improved in one way, though they have declined in another. The decline has been in the food. On my trip with Jack, I quickly learned that he was a road gourmet. He talked about the low quality of food at the franchise truck stops; they must think, he added, that drivers are too stupid to figure out how to get off the interstate. On our trip he often drove a few miles out of the way to get the sort of food that probably led to the folklore about eating where truckers eat. We stopped at three different spots of the same type, all small, older, wooden buildings, all serving good, inexpensive food, two of the three run by an older woman called "Mom." Once you've been to one of these little places alongside the old U.S. highways, Union 76 and Truck Stops of America will never look the same. Unless you hit one of the bad ones, of course, after which a franchised breakfast platter looks good.

Unlike Steve, Carl says the newer franchises, whose evolution Steve describes as a move toward the "glamorous," provide some improvements:

> Well, actually the truck stops were—hah, three quarters of them were pit stops, you know. Oh God, terrible. You never could find a decent place. If you found a place that had a shower, Christ, you'd have to steam-clean a shower before you could go in. So I used to just stop and rent a motel room and shower and shave. What the hell. A motel room cost about four bucks in them days, I guess, or two and a half. I forget any more. Truck stops were horrible.
>
> Now once in a while you'd—there was a lot of good eating places, you know. They were truck stops but they didn't sell fuel or anything, just strictly restaurants. They were nice. But then again in them days you could stop at a barbershop and almost all barbershops had showers, especially in the South.

Truck stops in the "old days," the story goes, had better food but worse facilities than those today. And of course, in the old days trucks often lacked sleeper compartments in the back, as Steve described earlier.

Other stories of olden times dramatize the difference between the old roads and the new interstates. During our trip to Chicago, Jack told me about the pre-interstate runs he used to make along old U.S. 40. Occasionally he would point to short stretches as the road came into view from our vantage point on the interstate. Usually they were narrow, winding, and full of steep hills. Following is another example of comments about the old highways from Steve:

> I don't know whether you ever ran the old roads back there or not. Well, I'll give you an example. One day—it was in June or July so I wasn't bothered with snow. It was thirty-nine miles from Hancock up here where [Route] 70 heads north towards Breezewood. From there to Cumberland is thirty-nine miles. Now I run this in the day-time in the summer and it took me three hours to do it. That's thirteen mile an hour, average. It was raining, summer rain showers. The old road where the tar bubbles up through the gravel. And I'd spin

40   *Independents Declared*

out on the rain going uphill. She'd spin. And of course going down the other side it would slide, you know. You had to go down slow to keep it from skidding on the same wet pavement. Three hours going thirty-nine miles. [reference to earlier story omitted]

The terrain back there—I brought a guy out of St. Louis one night. Incidentally, he ended up as a terminal manager or something for one of the big carriers up in Connecticut. I don't know how he did it because he was a real meatball. He was driving a truck out of St. Louis for AB Trucking. And I was at that time with Rockridge. So we're coming in up through Wheeling and Washington, Pennsylvania. And he says, "How are we going from here?" And I said, "Right straight over the hills." He says, "O.K., I'll follow you." Well he didn't know what we were getting into, but I'd been running that way. I knew it.

Well, between Washington and Uniontown there are a few hills, but right around Brownsville it's almost flat. And one of us had a headlight go out or something. I don't know what it was. And we pulled off on the shoulder of the road. He come up, he says, "Jesus, what hills. Where are you taking me?" I said, "We're not in the hills yet." He said, "It gets worse?" Said, "Yes it does." So I indoctrinated him that night. (I guess you did. It must be so much easier now with the interstate system, huh?) Unbelievable, unbelievable. Well the guy that's lost. He loaded in St. Louis yesterday, and he delivered Jessup—thirteen miles out of here—this afternoon. Then gets lost from Jessup coming to here.

The last "old days" road story is from Irv, and includes comments on traffic and accidents:

Yeah, I was going up the road one day—now, to start with you got to try to imagine the roads we ran those days. Now, you had U.S. 40, which is dual highway, running up into Delaware. You had two choices when you got into Delaware. You could cross the Pennsville Ferry, which is just about the location of the Delaware Memorial Bridge now. Or you could go to Chester and run the Chester Ferry. The Chester Ferry was cheaper. Most your companies routed the trucks across the Chester Ferry. They had a hot load they wanted to get there, they run you the Pennsville Ferry.

So when you got on the Jersey side you had two-lane highway, and you got up to I guess around Camden, around Westville, Camden. Some place up there you started hitting the four-lane highway. Above Westville, closer though to Camden, and you hit a four-lane highway. Well, that highway is a high-crown blacktop road, even though it was a divided highway. And it was a rat race when you got off them ferries, because everybody was jockeying, trying to get first. You get up around Linden, New Jersey, and all your trucks is scheduled to get in New York like early in the morning, like six or seven o'clock in the morning, right? That's why they leave their home terminal, in order to get up there. They figure them to get in there about that time.

So going through Linden one morning I'm going up there. It's a three-lane divided highway. And I had on a pretty heavy load. It was on a tandem. I guess maybe back in them days I had about thirty-two—thirty-three thousand. That was a heavy load. And those lights in Linden are timed for your north- and southbound traffic on [Route] 130. They have a long caution light, right? O.K., I'm approaching the intersection. I say maybe from twice as far as from here to that yellow post, which is what? Sixty feet. I'm maybe 120–150 feet away from it, the intersection. And this guy's coming up there beside me in the third lane. I'm in the center lane, he's in the third lane, out of Trenton with an empty trailer. And he jumped over in front of me and slammed on his brakes. In fact, he stopped, cross-blocking the intersection. And I could not get over in time, because I had to wait for a car beside me to get by before I could get over. Now, I couldn't stop in that distance so I had to go around him. I didn't quite make it. My fender just barely caught the back of his trailer. Well, it made a nice little crease in the fender.

Irv's description of the old roads was to provide background for an account of an accident that got him fired from his company-driving job, but it is useful here because of the detailed look he provides into pre-interstate road conditions. As with trucks and truck stops, road conditions make for an easier life now. Technology and the infrastructure have improved. The invisible web of regulations has not.

Regulation and Enforcement

While the scattered comments about trucks, truck stops, and roads are interesting reading, what mainly comes out of the "old days" discussions are the twin themes of regulation and enforcement. The general trend, according to the independents, is toward a thicker web of regulations and a greater chance that someone will be there to enforce them. Cal summarizes both these themes in a story about running to California:

Like I said, when I bought my first tractor and trailer—you won't believe this. We didn't have money to buy license plate. One year the plates come due. We didn't have money to buy them. I went to California and back with no license plates. Police didn't ride you to death then. But now, course, let's face it. It's a big industry. It's a big thing right now, trucking, compared to what it was. Like I said, when I started out I had a twenty-six-foot trailer. Then I got a thirty-foot trailer, and today they got forty-two-foot trailers, and wanting to go bigger. So it's like anything else. The police grew with it. And every state has found where they can get you. It don't matter. You can pick up the paper, and you know this well as I do. You can pick up the paper and if a state wants to raise a little extra money or something right away you'll see a piece in there—we're going to do this to the trucker. We're going to tax the trucker for this.

Cal points up the relationships among enforcement, regulation, and revenue. To obtain the latter requires regulations and a team to go out and fine the violators. Another passage from Carl's interview relies on the same logic:

Well shit, those regulations were—they weren't out looking like they are now, you know. You could make a trip—you could pull up the side of the road and lay yourself in the seat and take a nap. Didn't have to worry about somebody banging on the door wanting to, you know, "Let me see your permit." I mean, a lot of western states you had to have permits. Along the East Coast here they didn't do that until New York and Ohio started the ton-mile tax. That's how it all began. I think actually Ohio was the first. Then New York took it up, and then all the other states said, well, they do it. You know, we may as well do something like it. That's what started all that business.

The interviews contain plenty of other variations on the theme. Steve, for example, says there were regulations in the old days but little or no enforcement. Ike says during the war there were no scales and no officials around to bother you. There obviously were some regulations, but by and large nobody bothered the independent with them and they were not so directly intended to take a chunk out of his revenue. According to Carl, even hauling "hot" or illegal freight was less of a problem in the old days:

(Was it easier or harder to gypsy then?) Oh, it was easier. Like I say, states didn't have that many rules and regulations like they do now. You know, there was still lots of states that had regulation, but you know, they just wasn't out harassing you like they are now. I mean once in a while you'd get caught in Ohio. Ohio was always . . . for moonlight loads. That's the first thing they'd ask. "Let me see your bill of lading and who you're leased to." So if you had a load of freight on, either you had a bill of sale—it was your freight, or you dummied up the registration card to make it look like it was a company-owned piece of equipment, you know. Or you got fined twenty five, thirty dollars. You know, it wasn't much.

Once in a while one of them would bust you for a hundred, but that was a super-big fine. See, all they wanted to do was—they didn't want to kill you. They just wanted to extract a little bit off a lot of people. You know, a guy gets a fifteen, twenty dollar fine he ain't going to say much. But when you get fined four-five hundred dollars, you know, then you get grumbles, see. [comment on theft deleted]

> As I was saying, you know, in them days there wasn't as much
> harassment as there is now.

Carl starts out by saying that harassment was less in the old days,
then shifts into the counterexample of how officials would check
for hot freight, especially in Ohio. He describes two techniques to
avoid getting caught. One is to have a fake truck registration card
bearing the name of the shipper's company. If the shipper owns the
truck, then it is "private carriage," movement of its own goods by
a company not primarily engaged in the transportation business. A
second trick is to do a fake bill of sale, so that the independent
"buys" the load at the shipper's and "sells" it at the customer's. He
is then simply a person hauling his own property. These tricks are
several years old and well known by everyone in trucking. Contemporary hot freight techniques are discussed in chapter 4.

Another lesson in the old-days stories is a bit tangential but still
worth noting. There is a relationship between regulation and truck
technology that the outsider may not know. Steve describes it.

> Of course, in those days in the East—I'd say maybe from Kansas City
> east, or at least from the Mississippi River east, they were practically
> all four axles. You saw very few five-axle trucks in those days. There
> was no advantage to having a five-axle deal. Gross weights were low.
> Pennsylvania when I started was only forty-five thousand gross.
> That's tractor, trailer, and load. Yeah, there were a good number of
> companies that operated in Pennsylvania that only used three axles—
> you know, standard two-axle tractor and single-axle trailer—just
> because of Pennsylvania's weight law. New York State and Massa-
> chusetts—for years they used just three-axle trucks, but they used
> them with big rubber and loaded the hell out of them. They used big
> rigs, big wheels, and big springs, and just loaded them. They had odd
> gross weights too, but most everybody was overloaders.

The main point of Steve's description for present purposes is the
relationship between weight limits and number of axles (and length
of trailer, as Cal mentioned earlier). The length of trailer and number
of axles grows to adapt to improved highway construction and heav-
ier weight allowances. This is only one example of how trucks and
trailers have changed over the years in response to regulatory changes.
The transcript segments in chapter 9 indicate that tractor design is
in part a response to length limits.

The past, in short, was a better time by these accounts, because
regulations were simpler, enforcement was more lax, and fines were
lower. Although the technology of trucks and roads has improved,
the culturally spun webs of regulation thickened into a maze. In a
way, the independent truckers are just expressing their industry's

version of a general theme of our times—we live in an age of improved technology, but we struggle with an increasingly convoluted economic and regulatory snake pit. We have conquered nature and lost control of culture.

The Permanent Lease

One particular "old days" discussion is so critical to an understanding of the independents' working world that the rest of this chapter is dedicated to it. All of the independents who were active in the 1950s described a change that created the conditions for many of the issues they discuss. The change—a policy decision at the ICC—required independent truckers to lease on *permanently* with a single carrier. Before that decision, an independent could wander, and lease on for just a single trip to whomever he pleased. The most detailed description of this change, presented by Cal, is quoted at length:

> In 1945 I decided to try trucking. So I sold my car and scraped some money together and paid down on the first truck. Hauled produce out of Florida. Most anywhere you could trip-lease, or at that time you could trip-lease and get loads. You'd haul short runs for different companies out of Baltimore. You could run New York just about every night by trip-leasing to somebody. And the next day you'd trip-lease back for somebody else, whoever needed a truck. Which was a pretty good living because you could mostly pick your own loads. If one company had something that they didn't want to pay you enough, why, another company paid better; you could run whoever paid the best money. At least the companies had competition, because we wasn't tied to one company permanent. We could run for whoever we wanted to, whoever paid us the best, and therefore we made pretty good. [description of illness omitted]
>
> And, of course, about this time, why, the government come along and stopped us from trip-leasing. (When was that Cal, about.) I don't know the exact date when the government put the law into effect. You had to be leased to a company for thirty days at a time, and you could no longer trip-lease. That give the companies an edge on us, because they'd tell us what they wanted to pay, and we either took it or we didn't work. (Was this around say the '50s or something?) It was in the '50s, early '50s, I think, when this happened. And I just don't remember the dates anymore, but you can go to the court of the Interstate Commerce. They'll give you the exact dates because they got real rough on us about that.
>
> We'd sign a lease with a company for thirty days. And after they had us tied down for thirty days, then they'd tell us what they wanted to give us. We either took it or we left and didn't have nothing. And then finally they did get around to the point to where they would let us trip-lease back. And we had to have the check made to the company we were leased to for thirty days. And then they'd take

a percentage out of the check where we leased to another company. The amount of the trip was cut down in revenue to where it didn't hardly pay to even trip-lease back home. And, well, it just put a pressure on us to where you couldn't hardly make ends meet.

So the different guys kept fighting it. Fellow named Boster, he fought it for a while. And finally they got around to where the government started backing off a little bit on the leasing deal. And the guys more or less went to trip-leasing, having the checks made to them. They found a way of doing this and cut the companies out from taking the percentage two times, which give us a chance to make more money. So it finally got to the point to where [we] just wasn't making what we should of been making, and I leased permanent to a company.

The new policy pulled independents into a more controlled relationship with the for-hire carriers. Originally "you could pick your own loads"; if one carrier had no freight that paid enough to be worth the trouble then the independent just shopped around until he found one that did. Later in the interview, Cal describes how the process worked:

We were trip-leasing then to whoever we could get a load for. (So would you just get to know people in certain areas and then give them a call?) We had a list of numbers and we would call this list of numbers, which would be any companies that was operating. If we wanted to run New York, which in them days New York–Baltimore was a nice run because you could run it just about every night hauling tin plate. And then when they came along with the permanent leasing deal why that's—we used to get four to four-dollars-and-a-half a ton. And when they came along with the permanent leasing, why then they wanted to give us four-dollars-and-a-half a ton but we had to deadhead [run empty] back, or find a load and bring a load back through them, and give them a percentage of it. It just didn't pay.

Under the new rules, the carrier took on responsibility for the independent and his equipment on a permanent basis. The rationale for the change was more effective enforcement of safety regulations. The carrier got the "base plate" (home state license), was responsible for insurance, issued the permits (fuel, registration, and authority) for the different states he would run through, and assumed responsibility for safety of equipment and ability of the driver to operate it. (Usually the independent bore most of the expenses for permits and insurance.) The carrier also controlled the loads to which the independent could have access, the rate, and whether or not he could trip-lease to another carrier. Finally, the permanent lease carrier could take a percentage of whatever the independent made on a trip-lease to another carrier.

The details of this permanent lease relationship from the independent's point of view are discussed in the next chapter. The point here is that his market flexibility was reduced; no more hopping from carrier to carrier on a trip-by-trip basis. Some continued doing so for a while anyway, as Cal described. And some do so today, saying they are primarily "exempt" haulers when in fact they are not. Technically, a permanent lease could be terminated by either party the day after it was signed. In fact, untangling from the webs of one carrier and retangling with another was no longer a simple task.

If the carrier offered a load that was unprofitable or undesirable for other reasons, what choice did an independent have? Technically, as an independent contractor, he could always refuse to haul the freight, although independents tell stories about being fired for doing so. If he wanted to pull a load for another carrier, he could trip-lease, but only if it was allowed by his permanent lease carrier. (According to the ICC survey, 51 percent of the independents surveyed reported that their permanent lease carriers did allow trip-leasing.) If he could not trip-lease, he either pulled carrier freight, sat and waited, deadheaded (ran empty), or carried "hot" freight. Even if allowed to trip-lease, his payment usually came back through the permanent lease carrier, and the carrier often took a percentage of the money before it issued him a check (an average of 18.5 percent, according to the ICC survey).

Steve also describes the policy change and talks in some detail about the new version of trip-leasing:

> You went to that office and he got a load for you. And if he didn't have it—back then you could trip-lease to any of the carriers. It wasn't until—I guess it was the middle or late '50s that they came through with this no trip-lease at all. They brought the thirty-day lease through. An individual couldn't trip-lease to a carrier for less than thirty days, unless he was leased to another carrier. And then you had to do what they called "equipment interchange." You would lease your truck, which was in the name of one company, to another one. You didn't lease it as your truck. So that was for the purpose of getting back to a certain point.
>
> Whereas prior to that, before they brought out that thirty-day trip-leasing bit, there were lots of guys with a tractor and trailer. [description of trailers omitted] In those days you could go to any carrier. And what freight that they had that they didn't have their own trucks for, they would gladly put on you to get it hauled, usually at a tonnage rate. There were established tonnage rates between certain cities. Like they used to pay four dollars from here to New York. Four dollars a ton. Believe it or not, used to run from here to New York for forty—forty-five dollars.

Steve describes the same change that Cal did, though in a more neutral tone. He adds the technical term "equipment interchange" to describe the process where a permanent leased independent was "loaned" by one carrier to another; the independent did not do it himself. Steve also mentions the rule that a trip-lease was only to be allowed if the truck was returning to its home base.

Irv also describes the change, though, like Cal, he emphasizes the devastating economic consequences:

> Anyway, I was running freight with this one from Baltimore to New York. Well, this is about the time—when I got this other tractor is about the time that they passed that thirty-day lease law, where there was no more gypsying. You had to lease to a carrier for thirty days. (Well, this would be sort of the mid '50s or in there somewhere.) In the mid '50s, about '56, somewhere around through there. So it almost cured me from having a tractor, because I'm telling you it wasn't nothing like it was in the '40s. And I was just disgusted with the whole damned deal. You just couldn't make any money. You couldn't make the money like you could in the '40s. As an example, just talking to other guys that was in the business back in them days will tell you that them days you could make money, real money. But since the '40s you haven't been able to do it. It just ain't been there.

The final interviewee who was active during the period, Ike, had less to say about the permanent lease decision:

> So then everybody said it would be better to lease on to a company, instead of wildcatting and hauling produce, the exempt commodities. We couldn't get—the only thing we could get [was] other freight to haul back, but if they catch us with it on the truck then they would fine us. They said we couldn't haul no regulated freight. Well that's like it is today. (So they didn't start doing that till, say, in the early '60s or so?) No, early '50s. (Early '50s.) Yeah. See, as long as you were driving for a white man and all and they knew you were driving for him they wouldn't bother him so much, because if they did he'd go up there and raise hell.

Ike was hauling exempt commodities when the ICC's permanent leasing requirement was announced. He could haul them from an agricultural area to a population center, but then could not get a trip-lease to haul manufactured goods back. Ike leased on to a carrier, partly because with a white company official to front for him he found it easier to deal with authorities.

By the time I interviewed Irv I had identified a pattern in the independents' accounts of the permanent lease. Understanding the pattern required more information.

To the Archives

To get some background on this critical regulatory change, I went to the Interstate Commerce Commission library in Washington, D.C. There I found a record of hearings and deliberations that proved more complicated, and more instructive, than I expected.

All hell broke loose when the Motor Carrier Act of 1935 put the ICC into the truck regulation business. The ICC had no staff, no experience, and no budget. The ICC estimated that there were 325,000 for-hire trucks and 200,000 operators—roughly one-and-a-half trucks per operator—working on over a million miles of highway. With that kind of ratio, it is easy to believe what some of the histories say—that early trucking *was* independent trucking. As some ICC personnel summarized their undertaking at the time:

> It (ICC) realized that motor carriers, which far outnumber the railroads, are owned by single individuals, often poorly educated, and operated over short irregular routes, who must be taught the purposes, rules and penalties of the Motor Carrier Act before anything approaching efficient enforcement or universal compliance could be expected (De Felice et al. 1937:797).

To add to the madness, the Motor Carrier Act provided a "grandfather clause" whereby a motor carrier operating before 1935 could apply to get operating rights to continue. More than eighty thousand applications were filed (De Felice et al. 1937:799), and more than forty thousand of these were protested, mostly by railroads.

Many of the grandfather applicants, as one might guess, were independents, since so much of early trucking was just that. Right at the beginning, the ICC had to worry about the relationship between the regulated carriers that it was creating and the independents who drove the trucks that hauled the freight. The Motor Carrier Act did not give the ICC any authority to rule over leases, but an "administrative order" in 1937 gave the carrier "dominion and control" over the truck and driver and made the carrier responsible to the general public as well as the shipper of goods. In other words, the man might own and drive his own truck, but the carrier called the shots and assumed liability for damage. This order did not accomplish much; its main significance was to set up the precedent for the ICC to regulate leases later.

No sooner did the ICC get into the trucking business than World

War II broke out. As one participant in a congressional hearing later summarized, "It (trip-leasing) was encouraged during World War II by our Government as a means of utilizing to the utmost our trucking industry and highway system as a means of furthering the war effort" (U.S. Congress 1955:2). Indeed it was. In their postwar report, the Office of Defense Transportation (like their ICC predecessors) reported that at first blush trucking looked impossible to regulate (ODT 1946:101). They described their wartime problem—scarce resources (like rubber and gas) and a huge volume of freight to move. Their solution was to issue orders eliminating waste and to streamline the trucking industry. The essence of those orders was "no empty or partially loaded trucks allowed to move." Do what you have to do, said ODT, but run fully loaded. The emergent regulation of the industry, which had only just begun, was shelved in favor of another kind of regulation that demanded efficiency.

As the postwar dust settled, the ICC decided that trip-leasing had led to several "evils" so it began hearings in 1948 to develop regulations. In May of 1951 the ICC made four major recommendations, which are simplified here (ICC Reports 1952:722):

1. Leases must be at least thirty days in duration.
2. Lessee has exclusive possession (no subleasing).
3. Leased vehicle cannot be compensated by a percentage of the revenue.
4. The driver of the leased vehicle must be an employee of the carrier.

The four recommendations responded to two major problems with trip-leasing. The first was brought about by the carriers. After the war, the ICC reinstituted the old rules concerning carrier authority, and some carriers responded by using trip-leases to get around them. For instance, suppose that a carrier wanted to haul steel from Baltimore to St. Louis, but did not have the authority to carry steel to Missouri. To get around this regulatory problem, he could just trip-lease his truck to another carrier that did have the rights, in return for a small percentage of the revenue. This practice was called "red-dogging," because the directory of carriers and their rights was in a "little red book." By red-dogging, some carriers used trip-leases to essentially deregulate trucking. Needless to say, the ICC objected (not to mention some other carriers and the railroads).

The second problem addressed by the ICC in its recommendations was distinguishing between carriers who used independents and those who did not. General freight carriers, together with the railroads, argued for the new regulations; they claimed that the carriers who used independents had a "competitive advantage," since independents took care of all the expenses associated with truck, trip, and driver. Some carriers even used independents exclusively; they had authority but no trucks of their own.

The point is that the proposed leasing regulations were partly directed at *carrier* problems: they would restore regulation and even out the competition. The second set of problems did focus directly on the independents. Since they jumped from trip-lease to trip-lease, they were not adequately checked for compliance with safety regulations. The carrier provided them with proper identification for a trip, including any required by the states, and sometimes it was not returned. In the hearings, witnesses said that independents tended to overload and to damage the highways. And although they were covered by the carrier's insurance during a trip, between trips they were not necessarily covered. Independents were said both to work for nothing and to drive rates down, and to make so much money trip-leasing that the carriers could not hold them (1952:689).

Ten Teamster witnesses, all current or former independents, described how they drove more hours than they should, falsified logbooks, ran heavy, delayed repairs because of lack of funds, and coasted downhill (1952:691). The Teamsters were as interested in reducing the "competitive disadvantage" from nonunion freelance truckers as were the general carriers. One representative of an independent organization testified; he complained about required deposits, liability for damage claims, and the fact that carriers required that the vehicle title be assigned to them. His presentation is the only one that resembles the tone of current independent statements.

The announcement of the proposed regulations in 1951 was only the beginning of a long series of disputes. The final ruling, on an issue that began with hearings in 1948, finally came out in 1956. In the interim, the American Trucking Associations went to the Supreme Court, which ruled that the ICC did in fact have the right to regulate the content of leases. Agricultural interests lobbied for Public Law 957 that continued to allow exempt haulers to trip-lease after the exempt run. The carriers' lobby resulted in the ICC decision that carriers could trip-lease their trucks to each other after all, as long as they were heading toward a point where the carrier's authority would be in effect again. The public law also specified that the ICC had no right to tell anyone how to pay independents, so the percentage of revenue rule went too. The recommendation that drivers had to be employees was rejected as well; that would have ruined the flexibility of carriers who used independents and complicated situations in which an exempt hauler or independent from one carrier set up a trip-lease with another. But the thirty-day requirement stuck.

In its 1956 ruling, the ICC stated:

> In looking back to the inception of this proceeding, it is clear that the hard core of the problem confronting the Commission at that time and since has been the owner-operator trip lease and its attendant evils, such as widespread indifference to carrier responsibility, to safety of operations, and to the scope of carrier operating authority (1958:555).

How quickly they forget. Originally carriers were as much, if not more, of the issue as were independents.

Other data were presented over the years preceding the 1956 ruling suggesting that independents were not the safety problems described in the final recommendations. For example, in a legislative hearing, the president of the Machinery Haulers Association said its members, who relied heavily on independents, had received insurance reductions because of the independents' good safety record. He said they were small businessmen, some were college educated, and they were effective at handling the freight and taking care of their equipment. He reported that they earned between seventy-five hundred and ten thousand dollars a year (in 1956). They all preferred the percentage of revenue method of payment, he claimed, because it was clear to everyone; a mileage-based system required more records and sometimes led to disputes (U.S. Congress 1956).

Other favorable statements were made. An ICC survey in 1948, a six-month road check, found that leased vehicles had a slightly higher incidence of safety regulation violations, but except for the midwest region the differences were not statistically significant (ICC Reports 1952:694). The same report mentioned a study done by carriers who used independents; it showed no significant difference in accident rates between owned and leased vehicles, but the details of the study were not provided.

At any rate, by 1956 three of the four original rules were gone, largely because of lobbying from agricultural, trucking, railroad, and Teamster interests. All that remained was the thirty-day lease requirement, stripped of its impact on the agricultural exempt haulers and the trip-leasing of trucks between carriers. By 1956, independents had become the main target of the reforms. In a remarkable statement, the ICC explained its final decision:

> Still because of extensive litigation, pending legislation, consideration of special carrier problems, and vigorous opposition from some quarters of the industry, we have not made effective a rule to pro-

hibit or reasonably minimize the evils of the trip lease. Despite the continued opposition to such a rule, there is no longer good reason to continue its postponement (1958:556).

The leasing story does not end in 1956. Since the rise of the independent as a political force in the 1970s, the ICC enacted a "truth-in-leasing" provision designed to benefit him. (In fact, the cited ICC survey was conducted to gather information for that rule making.) But 1956 was a sea change in the world of independent truckers. The permanent lease set up the conditions for many of the issues discussed in the next several chapters. The intention was to reestablish economic regulation for the carriers and safety regulation for the independents; the results were primarily to regulate away the independents' autonomy in the marketplace of regulated freight.

The records of the hearings are a remarkable display of democracy as institutionalized conflict among competing interests; adversaries with differing degrees of political clout present their arguments in the face-to-face arenas of the courts and congressional and agency hearing rooms. Out of all the differences a policy emerges. The case also illustrates the devastating consequences for those without representation and power in those special arenas. The final policy accommodated all interests but the independents'. The primary negative consequences of the policy decision fell directly on them and it is not surprising that the interviews contain comments on these consequences. Now, of course, independents are present in those arenas, and recent legislation and rule makings reflect that presence, if not always to their satisfaction.

Chapter 4

Leases
and Loads

The Permanent Lease

Once the permanent lease was established in the 1950s, independents who primarily carried regulated freight had to enter into longer lasting, more complicated relationships with a single carrier. That situation set up the conditions for most of the problems talked about in the next few chapters. The permanent lease quickly became a focus of controversy. Wyckoff and Maister, describing it in the mid-1970s, noted that the document was typically full of duties and obligations for independents but sparse in those for the carrier (1975, chapter 6).

Since the mid-1970s, though, independents have become more of a political force. One direct result of their lobbying and testimony was the ICC survey cited throughout this book, commissioned to investigate problems with the permanent lease. Eventually, "truth-in-leasing" rules were enacted to protect independents. The details of the new rules are elaborate. For instance, among the "sample" of expense items to be described in the lease are: tractor and trailer maintenance, repairs, inspection fees, base license plate, other licenses, permits, fuel, fuel taxes, tolls, road taxes, withholding, social security, worker's compensation, fines, telegrams, telephone, identification on tractor and trailer, loading and unloading expenses, detention, pickup and delivery, cargo-collision-bodily injury-property damage-bobtail insurance, claims, credits on termination, trip-lease revenues, ancillary equipment, and empty miles (Maister 1980:91).

Under the new rules, the lease must also specify whether the items in this list will be charged to the independent directly, paid by the carrier and then deducted from the independent's check, or paid by the carrier outright. An independent's pay may be based on a percentage of the revenue, a fee per mile, a fee per ton, a fee per "move," or anything else the independent and the carrier agree on. Some of the teachers' stories reveal that the leasing rules provide no absolute safeguard. The dwindling ICC staff can only go after the big sinners (if they can convince the equally understaffed Justice Department to prosecute). And most independents have neither time nor money for a civil suit that will cost more (including their job) than they can possibly gain.

Little wonder that Steve cited the advantages of one job where he simply hauled company trailers from one terminal to another—fewer lease-type items to worry about. In that job, incidentally, Steve was paid by the mile. Other jobs (especially in the old days) paid by the ton. But the typical method of payment (reported by three-quarters of the ICC survey respondents) is payment by a percentage of the rate, usually around 75 percent if the independent provides the trailer, and maybe 10 percent or 12 percent less if he does not. Two of the interviewees, Phil and Irv, other independents, and the ICC survey report these percentages.

Does the independent have no control at all? Well, as contractor rather than employee, he can in principle refuse to take the freight, though the principle is not always honored. Steve tells a story about the time ABC wanted him to load hazardous material. Since it was illegal to carry explosives through the tunnels on the turnpike, he refused. The trip over secondary mountain roads would have taken too much time and produced too much wear and tear on the tractor. ABC fired him.

If a carrier consistently abuses independents, word gets out, and the carrier will have trouble finding and holding them. In fact, "turnover" (characterized as a "number-one problem" from the carrier's point of view by Maister) provides a handy statistic to evaluate carriers. The ICC survey showed that one-third of the independents had been in their present lease for a year or less. An example from Will's interview shows how carrier reputation is discussed:

> There's an outfit that called me Friday that I was thinking about going to work for. I understand they're pretty decent. Now they were a bad outfit, but apparently they found the error of their ways. Take Mark Transport that I worked for, for instance. When they started cutting their rates and they lost their drivers they probably had about twenty guys working for them at one time when I worked down there. Then as the work started tapering off they drifted off into other directions. Now if Mark runs an ad in the Baltimore paper for an owner/operator and a guy calls in, as soon as you say it's Mark

Transport they'll hang up on you. The owner/operator don't even want—they wouldn't go to work for them for nothing. You know they just have such a bad name.

(What did this company you mentioned do to change their ways?) Which one? (Oh, you just said you were talking to some other company.) Well, they had a low rate. Apparently they were starting to go under. They had company-owned equipment also. They sold a lot of their company equipment and started treating the owner/operators better. I think they raised their rates—maybe not raised their rates, but they raised the percentage to the owner/operators. They have their own fuel pump. They help the guys out with repairs, let them charge it to the company and pay it back, you know. They've really gone out of their way in order to revitalize their company. And they're starting to come back again where they're getting good business. They got a lot of good people working for them. But that's the only one that I know of that's done it, or had sense enough to.

The independent checks the reputation of the carrier if he knows what he is doing and if he has been in the business long enough to ask the right questions. But in the end, once he signs on he is tangled with the carrier through licenses and permits, insurance, and several other things, right down to the company signs on the side of his tractor door. Usually, most of the operating costs are his, and a percentage of his revenue is the carrier's. The next passage, from Jack's interview, describes the feelings that this situation can inspire:

Well they found out it's cheaper. Hell. I mean it don't cost them nothing. Don't cost them a damn thing for an owner/operator. I mean the only thing they're doing is making telephone calls for you. What else are they doing? They're putting insurance on you and you're paying for that. [family exchange deleted] Hey, they getting 25 percent for what? What are they getting 25 percent for, huh? You explain what they're getting 25 percent for. You go to a broker, a broker only takes 10 percent of the gross load. And a common carrier takes 25. Well a lot of them take 28 percent now. All your union carriers take 28 percent, and it don't pay you to run a union carrier. It don't pay you to run for them. You do better running a nonunion carrier than you do a union carrier.

(What do they do with that 25 percent? Supposedly they pick up your insurance. They do your paperwork on the permits and all that kind of stuff. Is that right?) Some of them do. (Some of them do. But they don't all do that.) Now ABC they don't do nothing. I got to fight and scream and everything for my fuel tax stickers on the side of my truck, and I still ain't got half of them. And I pay for them. I got to pay for that. Union carriers they pay for them, but I pay for everything on ABC. (So even if they do the paperwork you still get stuck with the bill?) Yeah, yeah, still got to pay for all of them. So they get

25 percent for nothing in my opinion, you know. I mean I don't know what the hell they're doing that deserves 25 percent.

(I've been trying to figure that out ever since I've been talking to owner/operators.) You know, I mean they do carry the liability insurance on the truck when you're loaded. That's all. Only when you're loaded. When you're empty you fall back on what they call a bobtail insurance. I got to carry that. (That's yours.) Yeah, that's my responsibility then. But hey, I mean, Jesus, when they got me covered I got a couple hundred dollar load on for them, you understand. They're getting 25 percent of that. (Do they provide the cargo insurance too?) Yeah they got to carry—you know, you don't know about that damn insurance. If you turn around and damage it, I'm responsible for the first five hundred dollars in damage on a union carrier. On a non-union carrier I'm not sure. I think it goes up to maybe like five thousand dollars I might be responsible for. I'm not sure. (They don't tell you that.) No, they don't tell you that. No, they don't tell you that till after it happens.

See, I'm responsible for it. Anything that's on that truck I am responsible for. I am. That's mine until I give it to the man that signs for it. It's my freight, and I'm completely responsible for that goddamn freight on there. [story about insurance payments deleted] And then they coming up with this here if they can prove, what do you call it—negligence on the driver's part—I can be responsible for the whole amount then, if they can prove negligence on me. I'm responsible for everything. Then they can come back—you know the insurance company pays off, but the insurance company comes back on me, see. And they can turn around and take my house. They can take my truck. They can take everything I ever worked for all my life they can take away from me.

It doesn't sound fair, although the carriers' side of the story has not been heard. Maister, describing the carriers' management problems, claims that 25 percent is not exorbitant; at least, he argues, carriers benefit less than the shippers. On the other hand, the carrier does get a fleet with no employee or equipment maintenance problems. The independent, in return, gets access to freight, permits, and paperwork. The services that the carrier provides are valuable, and are characterized that way by some independents. Some even say they prefer the permanent lease because they do not want to deal with state and federal paperwork and hustling for freight. Their reasons will be apparent in stories of the trials and tribulations of getting authority.

In addition, the carriers that independents usually lease on with certainly were not getting rich during this study; the average operating ratio (expenses divided by revenues) for specialized commodity carriers was 98 percent in 1982. The trade journals described several business failures during the period. I do not know what the carrier's fair share of the gross load would be, nor what rationale underlies the 25/75 split. I do know that Dan said he planned to use his authority to lease on other independents; he and his wife were trying to figure out a fair deal and thought that they should take 10 percent to 15 percent for the loads and the paperwork. That is the broker's approximate cut in Jack's story, a broker in this context being the person who finds exempt agricultural loads.

Despite the problems with the permanent lease, independents want to carry this regulated freight and the permanent lease is now the primary way they can get it. Whatever happened to the trip-lease? It didn't disappear; it just became part of the relationship with the permanent lease carrier.

Trip-Leases and Loads

Although those who primarily hauled exempt goods could still trip-lease to get back home, the independents who mostly hauled regulated freight saw the trip-leasing life disappear in the 1950s. But remember that the carriers lobbied and modified the rules so that they could trip-lease their own trucks to one another, as long as the purpose of these trips was to get the trucks back to areas they could legally serve. A new logic appeared—an independent permanently leased to a carrier now could trip-lease only with the carrier's consent. In the next passage, Will describes what happens if the carrier does not allow trip-leasing and the freight is running slow.

> Now see, that was the same thing with Piedmont Trucking out of North Carolina. Now that's a good company to work for. They treat you good. Management's nice. But I left here like a Sunday night and I went from here to Waynesboro, Virginia, and from Waynesboro they paid me to deadhead over to Richmond, which is beautiful. And from Richmond up to Massachusetts. O.K., that's Tuesday morning. I got nine hundred dollars made, right? Which is great. Beautiful week going. I sit up there from Tuesday—Wednesday. Thursday morning I says, "Pal, I ain't sitting here no longer." They didn't have no freight. And why they couldn't get something—why they don't have more freight out of a town as big as Boston, and when I say Boston, that's I'd say, within a hundred miles of there. That included parts of New Hampshire and Maine and everything. Anyway, finally Thursday I said, "I can't sit here no more." So they said O.K. This is when the new fuel surcharge thing [see below] went into effect, which wasn't that long ago. They used to give us twenty-five cents a mile when you deadheaded over two hundred miles. So I asked the guy on the telephone when he told me to go from Boston down to New Jersey, which is about 350 miles. I says, "Well, do I get the twenty-five cents a mile?" He says no. He says, "You only get the fourteen cents

a mile now that the new surcharge is in." So right there I took a cut, you know. So I says alright.

Well I was at a motel for a couple days up there, and my truck was broken into and everything. So I said the heck with it. I'll just leave and go on down there. I know I'm only ninety miles from home. And if I get mad there I can go home. Anyway, by the time I drove down there—when I got there they got four guys waiting for loads. This is Thursday afternoon, so I know I can't get a load Thursday night. It'd either be Friday morning or Saturday. This trip's put me on next week's check. I still wound up in the hole. Out on the highway for seven days with the nine hundred dollars. If I could of trip-leased out of Boston I could have had a load the next day. But when you're under permanent lease you can't trip-lease unless they allow it, and the majority of them won't. They want you sitting so they can service their customers, you know. There's no other way to go. So anyway, I got to Jersey and I seen those four guys waiting. I just left them a note that I broke down, and I came on home.

That is the problem. Will describes the carrier as "nice people" that "treated you good." But the carrier will not allow its independents to trip-lease. As Will says here and later, "they got to service their customers," even if it means the independent sits for a few days away from home earning no revenue. That is one reason some carriers prohibit trip-leasing, a legitimate reason from the viewpoint of carrier profitability. They want their independents available to meet increases in demand from shippers.

Will gets stuck in Boston—no freight and he cannot trip-lease. Piedmont sends him to New Jersey to another terminal, but he has to "deadhead" or run empty to get there. Worse yet, he is affected by a new fuel surcharge.

Understanding the surcharge requires some background knowledge. Most readers will recall the independent truckers' shutdown in the late 1970s. Its cause was partly the dramatic increase in the price of fuel. In response to the protest, the ICC invented a program to compensate independents for the increasing costs. Originally, the compensation was based on a percentage of the freight rate, but in 1982 it changed to cents per mile. (In a 1983 article I analyze the arguments for and against the change that were presented at an ICC hearing. The entire program was recently tossed out by the courts.) Will stated that Piedmont used to pay independents twenty-five cents a mile if they deadheaded over two hundred miles. Now Piedmont tells Will he gets the new supplement instead—fourteen cents instead of twenty-five cents. At the Jersey terminal, Will sees he is fifth in line late on a Thursday, gives up, and goes home.

Independents tell many stories like this—no trip-lease allowed and a choice between sit-and-wait or deadhead. (The ICC survey found that independents run empty about 26 percent of the time.) The problem can be more exasperating if the carrier has company trucks as well as leased independents, as Red describes.

> (You said in the first one you had to deadhead home a lot, right?) Yeah, they just didn't have any accounts up in that area. That was part of the problem. They didn't have too many accounts in eastern Pennsylvania and New Jersey. And the second problem up in there was what freight they could get, in addition to having a bunch of owner/operators leased to them they also had company-owned trucks driven by employees. And, oh, I don't think I need to go into a whole great big explanation as to who got what freight was available. And we got what was left over.

This is not the only time Red or others (like Will) talk about independents getting "the leavings." If the carrier is paying to maintain a fleet, then the freight will tend to go to its own trucks rather than to leased trucks on which it gets only 25 percent of the revenue. Once again, what is logical for carrier profitability is detrimental to the leased independent.

Another of Will's stories is a bit more favorable to carriers:

> Well, they're a decent company. They didn't hassle you. They had plenty of work, you know. The railroad has plenty of work. (Would they let you trip-lease, Will?) Well, as a matter of fact when they don't have work, they'd get a load for you and they don't take any percentage of it. (They don't take any?) No. They take absolutely nothing. I went to Rochester, General Motors. I was supposed to drop a load there and pick up a load coming back from the same place. Well, I broke down on the way up and they shipped my load that I had waiting on me. So the company called over Buffalo, got me a trip-lease, rented pallets for me, which is on a pallet exchange. I guess it didn't cost them nothing. They exchange them someplace up and down the road. And got me the load. And once I went to the other carrier and signed a trip-lease agreement with him, all of it was in my name. And they paid me directly. My company took absolutely nothing.

The carrier, working "intermodally" with the railroad, found Will a trip-lease when he broke down; not only that, it did not take a cut of his revenue. The carrier even arranged for pallets, wood frames on which the freight is stacked so that a "towmotor" or forklift can move them around. Most carriers require the trip-lease check to be issued to them; they take a percentage and then pass on the remainder to the independent.

Will talked about the usual practice of taking a cut of the trip-lease in the very next segment of his interview:

> Some companies take 10 percent. When you trip-lease you still only

Independents Declared

get a percentage. Say they got 75 percent. Well, I was on 65 percent. When I trip-leased with Piedmont they gave me 80 percent of the 75 percent that they got. Which, you know, I did that one week and the guy trip-leased me a load of beer out of North Carolina. And I'd run a load of paper. I really run good that week. I had hardly any deadheading miles at all, right? The dispatcher says to me—you know, one thing I think about this dispatcher. I feel in my heart that he was waiting for a couple owner/operators to offer him money to work them a little better. I really believe that. Anyway I really run good that particular week. And he said, "Boy, you really made a lot of money this week." Man, when I got that check and I seen how they cut these trips up when you trip-lease. You know there wasn't nothing left. I don't even know if I made fuel money. I was so sick from looking at it. I didn't even figure it out hours against miles, you know.

Piedmont takes 20 percent of the independent's trip-lease money before it passes on the check. Its cut is only a bit higher than the 18.5 percent average reported in the ICC survey.

Will mentions a central person in independent trucking life— the dispatcher. Maister, describing dispatchers as key figures to both the carrier and the independent, quotes one of his carrier interviewees:

> The key men in any operation are the dispatchers. To drivers they are the company. They should have the patience of Job, the wisdom of Solomon, and a damned good sense of humor. We expect them to be the driver's buddy and father confessor all rolled into one (1980:98).

Maister adds to this list such attributes as honesty, fairness, and a knowledge of independent trucker profitability. He also notes that from a carrier point of view, the dispatcher is the main person finding, organizing, assigning, and monitoring the delivery of freight.

In Will's story, the dispatcher is not handing out a fair share of high-rated loads. Will, for unspecified reasons, thinks he wanted a payoff for good freight. True or not, it is clear that Will's sense of that carrier is largely shaped by the behavior of his dispatcher. In later stories from the interviews and my trips, dispatchers appear in positive and less complimentary lights. They appear, because for the independent, they usually *are* the company.

In his interview, Red described a carrier that always provided trip-leases, because it was one company in a conglomerate.

> (Red, when you were running out of Texas were you always carrying their loads or were you doing trip-leasing?) Most of the time we were running their loads. When we would go to California—that particular company had very limited ICC authority eastbound from California, so we would trip-lease. They would arrange a trip-lease for us. Well,

that particular company was a subsidiary of a trucking conglomerate which is based in Chicago. Smith Enterprises actually is the—my company was just one of the trucking companies. Smith Enterprises is the whole blanket thing. It's owned by an ex-doctor. And I've heard different reports. Some people say he owns over a hundred different trucking companies, but I know he owns a whole flock of them. But anyhow, we had a couple of companies that had authority out of the West that were all part of the same conglomerate that we would trip-lease to. (So you sort of stayed within the family that way.) Yeah, yeah, always within the family. But that was one of the things they did for us. They always lined us up a load.

Red's carrier does not fit the traditional characterization of the independents' part of trucking as a market shared by a large number of comparatively small companies, though this picture is changing with deregulation. As Red tells it, there are underlying patterns of ownership that work to his own advantage. Within the conglomerate are several different carriers serving as resources in the quest for freight. Red favorably evaluates the company because it "always lined us up a load."

Later in his interview, Red brought up another reason why carriers might avoid dabbling in trip-leases: insurance liability. When an independent, permanently leased to one carrier, takes a trip-lease from another, which one is liable? Red describes one way that the problem can get passed on to an independent:

A lot of times when you trip-lease to a carrier there'll be a "hold harmless" clause in the lease, usually written in very fine print, usually written in legalistic jargon that the average trucker can't understand. And often times, particularly in the last six or eight years, this has come more into the—it's become public knowledge and been a subject of much discussion, whether these trip-lease carriers ought to be held liable. Truckers would go ahead and trip-lease and I know I've done this myself a hundred times or more. You go ahead and trip-lease anyhow, even knowing that you could be held responsible, for the simple reason you need a load. And the only way you're going to get one is to just go along with the conditions, again because you have no leverage. And we've tried over the years to get the Interstate Commerce Commission to do something about that. And that's one thing that they just have never gotten—they don't seem to be willing to bite that bullet, you know, and really put these carriers under the gun.

(So legally when you're on a trip-lease all that stuff isn't covered.) On some leases. Now, for instance, with this carrier here. When you trip-lease for them my understanding is—which I've never trip-leased for them. But my understanding is that they cover a trip-leaser on public liability, property damage, and even cargo damage. And I've found that the more ethical carriers will do this.

In the next segment, Red tells a story from his own experience describing the problems that can result if a "hold harmless" accident occurs.

Control through Leasing

The permanent lease allows the carrier to control trip-leasing in a number of ways. Most difficult for the independent, the carrier may simply prohibit it. Under those conditions, an independent must deadhead (with or without mileage payment) to get to the freight, or sit and wait until freight appears. Deadheading and waiting around may be even more prevalent if the carrier has its own fleet of company trucks to keep moving as well. Obviously, when the truck is not loaded and moving an independent is not making money. Even if a carrier does allow trip-leasing, it will probably take a percentage of the percentage before passing on the money.

With this kind of control, it is not difficult to imagine what may happen if the independent annoys the carrier. Jack talked about a case in which a carrier punished him for his self-described "rabble-rousing":

> See, one day I went up to Maine from out of Boston. I deadheaded up. And when I got up there, we had a jockey stayed up there, and he loaded the trucks. Tarped them, because these were eight-foot loads with eight-foot tarpaulins that we had to carry—we bought and paid for. They cost like six-seven hundred dollars, the tarps did. Had eight-foot drops on them, and they would cover a forty-foot trailer. And you had to lace them up in front, lace them up in the back and everything. I was pulling this insulation board and stuff like this all over the country, you know, all over the East Coast here. And I got up there and I waited around till Friday, and they didn't have nothing. I had been trip-leasing to Deacon Brothers down in New Hampshire, where I was tripping out of all the time. And when their trucks would get down here to Baltimore—this Deacon Brothers is a different outfit than Bay Transport, see. And they would bring lumber down, and then they would trip themselves back through Bay Transport back up to New England. So they had a pretty good thing going there, you know, between the two companies. Bay Transport and Deacon Brothers. So they would trip me back a lot of times. I got a lot of loads back through them. And then Bay Transport found out that I was tripping myself through Deacon Brothers, see.
>
> And then one day when I was up there I told the jockey if the company went looking for me—I had called Deacon Brothers up. And

they told me they had a load of lumber sitting up there going right in to Washington, D.C. And I said, "Good." And I said, "I'll be right down." That was 350 miles I had deadheaded out of Maine to New Hampshire. And when I pulled in there, the jockey had told the dispatcher. They called up looking for me, and he had told him that I had left up there. So they in turn called up and told Deacon Brothers not to trip me, that they would not release me. And when I walked in the office down there ready to get loaded the man told me, he said, "I'm sorry Jack, I can't load you." I said, "What do you mean you can't load me?" He said, "Bay Transport called me up and told me that they would not release you, and that we can't trip you."

I went down to White River Falls Junction, above Vermont, which was—see the place was right there at the state line. And I went down there and I called up. I was using three telephone booths. I had the union on one, I had Washington, D.C. on the other one, and I had Bay Transport on the other one. And I mean I had a three-way conversation going. And I mean we were doing some mighty tall cussing back and forth. And I be threatening to kill everybody I got my hands on that day. Oh, I was mad. And I wound up deadheading out of there back to Baltimore. That was not only deadheading, you know, 350 miles out of my way plus another 500 and some miles—or almost 600 and some miles back home. It was almost a thousand miles I deadheaded myself, because Bay Transport wouldn't release me.

Jack eventually left this carrier to sign on with another. Not surprising is that the main reason he picked the new carrier is because it does not control when, where, or how the independent trip-leases, as long as he runs one of its loads a month. Later segments reveal that Steve and Carl have also changed carriers to avoid deadheading, although their stories are not as dramatic as Jack's. As he characterized the job with Bay Transport, Jack said, "so being an independent, forget it. You're not. You're actually a company driver even though you're paying for the goddamn truck."

Jack's current carrier is an exception (not to mention illegal). Most carriers want as much control over the independent's truck as they can get. Maister characterizes the problem of control as the "greatest disadvantage of using owner/operators" (1980:41). The independent's stories reveal that high turnover can be as much a comment on the carriers as it is on independents. Red told a story during our trip together about testimony he gave at a hearing. When questions were raised about his changing carriers so often, he compared

Independents Declared

himself to Diogenes, wandering the land in search of an honest carrier.

Alternatives to the Lease

If the permanent lease carrier has so much control, why do most independents lease on? The permanent lease carrier does take responsibility for much technical, time-consuming paperwork, and a good one keeps its independents moving because it finds loads. Besides, what are the options? The independent can be exempt, illegal, or get his own authority. Exempt I did not learn much about. It appears to be a different world. But the other two possibilities, running illegally or getting one's own authority, did come up in the interviews.

"Hot freight," as the name suggests, is anything that should not be on the truck. (Hot freight is different from "hot loads," freight that has a "rush" delivery request.) It is not called "hot" because it is stolen; it is hot because the independent does not have the ICC authority to carry it from where he picks it up to where he takes it. The independent can find hot freight any number of ways. One way is to go to an agent or broker who is known to handle it on the side. Another way is to go to one of the truck stops around the country known to attract brokers who specialize in hot freight.

On one trip I spent some time at one such truck stop. The place was littered with small offices where brokers coordinated loads with trucks. I did not fully understand the situation when we left Baltimore, but when I was told to "keep your mouth shut and pretend you're learning the business" I started to get the idea. By the ethics of my profession, research had just gone into questionable status; but I decided that, though I am fond of my professional association, I had no intention of dying for it.

I learned as much as I could in our short stay. (I also learned that hell for a researcher is an interesting place where you can't ask any questions.) Apparently the brokers work under the pretense of the "shipper cooperative." To simplify, such a cooperative is set up when a group of manufacturers get together and purchase a fleet of trucks that they use cooperatively to deliver their own goods. Since this is private carriage, it is not regulated by the ICC. The hot freight trick is that the "cooperatives" are assembled on the spur of the moment, depending on the trucks that are around and the shippers that have freight. The general idea is that the independent makes more money than he would with the traditional share of the revenue; the shipper saves a little over what a regulated carrier would charge; the hot freight broker takes his cut; everybody comes out ahead. Apparently this arrangement, and others like it in different parts of the country, have been around for years.

Shortly after we arrived, we went from office to office looking for "pieces." (In legal trucking, one talks about assembling "LTLs," less-than-truckload shipments, into a load; in the world of hot freight, one talks of "pieces.") By evening, we still were short of a full load, so the independent decided to stay the night. After wandering around with him and a couple of his friends for a while, I took off on my own.

On the general principle that deviance clusters, it did not surprise me that in this truck stop I was offered illicit chemicals three times, stolen tools out of a car trunk twice, and stolen everything out of a van once. The independent slept on a couch in a friend's office. I stayed in the sleeper and listened to hookers "pounding the paint off the door" all night. This truck stop was, however, atypical. Truck stops range from down-and-out to downright wholesome; most, though, were like most small towns—deviance is available if you care to seek it out, but it will be discreetly kept out of sight (though it is sometimes noisily advertised on the CB).

Working through brokers is one way to get hot freight, or as Dave put it, to be "an outlaw, renegade, gypsy-type truck driver." Another way is to develop a continuing relationship with a shipper. Cal spent several years doing so:

(How did that come about, hauling directly for the shipper, back in those days?) Well, they approached me one time about hauling some local freight for them, railroad sidings and all, and paid me so much an hour. And then in the meantime, why, I just worked around to where they started talking about this freight that they were shipping to California and South Carolina. I used to haul aluminum floors for computer rooms. It's an elevated flooring, they call it. 'Course since that time they don't make that anymore, or at least the same man doesn't make it anyhow. But I hauled for them for quite a while. And I done good with them, until finally the government stepped in. The freight companies started complaining, I was told. And the government stepped in and told me it was an illegal operation. I could no longer do it. The aluminum company tried to tell them I was giving them better service than the carriers give them. And I was doing a better job for them. But they still said it was illegal. The only way I could do it was be on the company payroll.

And at that time—to show you the way the government operates, they took me to court and Harris even made the remarks that he was going to put me out of business. The Interstate Commerce man. We had a big fight in the courtroom because he tried to lie on me and we had a go-around. They published an article about me. I still fought them, and at no time did they ever really find me guilty. They just asked me whether I would plead guilty to eight counts and pay an eight-hundred-dollar fine. They would drop everything. So after I did this Harris said that he was coming out to my house and he was going to inspect my trucks and put me out of business. And 'course at the time I threatened him if he ever come to my house I'd stomp him in the mud. And he never did come to my house. And to this day I've never had a word with the man. I've never run into him.

(What was your argument against him in the court? How did you argue against him?) Well, my argument was it was taking my rights away from me. I had a right to work and make a living, which the government later on passed a law, a right-to-work law. And the government claims that I just wasn't allowed to drive my own truck. To this day I can't see no law or nothing that should forbid me from driving my own truck and hauling your merchandise as long as I got the qualified insurance. I had the qualified insurance. I carried insurance on the other guy the same as myself. They couldn't get nothing on me. They claim that the only reason they took me to court was on driving my own truck on the eight counts they wanted me to plead guilty to. They had me for they said a hundred at the time, but they would drop it to eight. They didn't really have a strong case. It was just that the harassment that they caused to the company, that the company decided they wouldn't go along with it anymore because it was too much harassment. Every day they'd be out at the company seeing whether one of my trucks was backed in there or something. And we just got to the point we had to give it up.

Cal hauled directly for the shipper for several years, building up a fleet of several trucks in the process. His only complaint about the situation (a recurrent theme in his interviews) was that he had no health and welfare benefits. But the arrangement was pure hot freight. To be legal "private carriage" the shipper has to own or lease the trucks and the drivers must be company employees. The trucking companies complained to the ICC and the agency came after Cal, as he describes here and elsewhere.

Carl, one of the drivers who worked for Cal during this period, was also interviewed. He talked about how he got into the job and then described in more detail how they got caught:

Well, what it was, all these carriers were getting all kinds of freight, you know. And all of a sudden the freight stopped. The carriers send their salesman around to see why they lost the freight, and they see Cal's two trucks or three trucks back in there. They write this down. They file a complaint with the ICC. (He didn't have a certificate.) That's right. He wasn't a certified carrier. So they fined him a couple of hundred bucks, and we quit hauling for the aluminum company. And then that's when he sold me the truck and then we just started gypsying again, hauling anything we could get, anywhere we wanted to go.

Cal's story is the longest tape-recorded description of hot freight, but there are others. Dan, for example, described how through informal networks in his hometown he arranged a deal with a local shipper and entered into a steady relationship something like the one Cal had with the aluminum company.

In general, drawing from interviews and conversations, it sounds like most independents haul hot freight occasionally, sometimes because there is no other way to get a load. Some actively seek it out, either working through brokers or establishing a more stable relationship directly with a shipper. Those who talked about hot freight most openly emphasized the improvement in their economic situation when compared to leasing to a carrier. Ike talked about "hauling moonlight, hot freight, any kind of freight I could get in my trailer. That made more money than what the company was paying me." Dan told a similar story:

(So you were saying then that you were initially hauling the stuff at the mine without the authority, right?) Yeah, without the authority. I was using the company's license plates, the people that I was leased to, using their plates and their name up and down the road. But I would say there's quite a few guys that run up and down the road here. The only way they can make it is hot freight it, as they call it. You just can't make it with a company anymore. That 25 percent off the top is actually your profit that they're putting in their pocket. It's just one of those things. Yeah, you know, get out on your own. You get what you want and to hell with the other guy.

I mean, that's why I started my own authority, and all this shit that we're going through to get that authority is ridiculous as far as I'm concerned. I made phone call after phone call after phone call and lawyers' fees and all this other crap. And you think you can start driving in these goddamn states and you can't. They give you a ticket because you don't have the authority to run in their goddamn state. Well, what the hell good is ICC authority if you got to start going to every state for authority and all this other crap.

Dan hauled hot freight regularly, even while he was permanently leased. He just told the carrier that he deadheaded home, and then used company plates and cab identification to look legal out on the road. But Dan (like Ike) moved from hot freight to an application for his own authority after the Motor Carrier Act of 1980 simplified the application process for independents.

I spent an evening at Dan's house learning about the application process from his wife. In Dan's family, like that of most independents I have worked with, the man drives the truck and the woman runs the business and keeps the books. Dan's wife described how their federal authority was approved, once she learned to tell "the right lies" and located and paid the relevant experts. But the real problems began when she started to deal with the states. Most states require registration, state authority, and fuel tax permits. Some also require filing for the increasingly popular "third structure" taxes on ton/ miles run in the state. She showed me the forms she was currently working on for two western states—the forms for application, not the other forms for quarterly report filings. It took me about an hour to comprehend them. States often require posted bonds and local business addresses, and some (but not all) participate in one or more registration reciprocity schemes with some (but not all) others. I have met independents who get their authority but still work through hot freight brokers or directly with shippers; they see the authority as a potential help if they are checked during a trip, but they do not have the time or money or know-how to get straight with all the states. (The problem of state differences recurs in chapter 9.)

Since the passage of the Motor Carrier Act of 1980, getting ICC authority is easier, but the states still set up difficult barriers. And once the independent gets legal standing with the states, he has the problem that so concerns Will—getting enough cash reserve in place so that he can do without carriers providing the cash advances for trips and repairs.

If the independent rules out hot freight and getting his own authority, exempt is the only remaining alternative to permanent leasing. An exempt hauler, of course, still has to have the relevant state permits, and he will often trip-lease after hauling agricultural goods to an urban center. Leased independents also carry an exempt load from time to time. On two of my long-distance trips we brought exempt loads back to the East from agricultural areas in the Northwest and Southwest. But exempt hauling is a style of independent trucking I did not explore.

Most independents—all the ones I worked and talked with— depend for loads on a permanent lease carrier. In this style of independent trucking, the independent signs the lease and checks in with the dispatcher. But once he is offered a load (of the legal sort), his share is usually based on a percentage of a rate, usually quoted as so much money per hundred pounds of freight. The problem is that as a permanently leased independent trucker, he has no control over what that rate might be.

Chapter 5

Rates

Rate Madness

Rates are something else again. An examination of their historical evolution, their bureaucratic implementation, and the activity around them in the current era of deregulation would yield another book to accompany this one. Fortunately, the burdensome details are not necessary here, but a few crucial facts need to be understood.

First, and most important, rates are set by the carriers, not by the independents. The relevant question for an independent is simply "What's the rate"; the choice is to take it or leave it. Second, under deregulation it is easier than ever before to lower rates. The old system, where regional bureaus and the ICC kept a lookout on rates, is for all practical purposes dead. Realistically, carriers can now do as they please. Third, deregulation also established a new policy called "eased entry"; it is simpler now to get authority to haul more commodities over larger areas. Fourth, during the early 1980s, the U.S. economy was undergoing a recession or depression, the choice of term being a function of one's commitment to euphemisms. The result of all this—greater rate flexibility, more carriers, and a recession—was an economic squeeze on carriers that pressured them to lower rates. Trade publications such as *Transport Topics* and *Heavy Duty Trucking* reflected the confusion of the era as many carriers scrambled for survival while others went under.

Before the deregulation era began, rates were more stable, but equally senseless. The literature on the trucking industry describes the madness, including the confusion right at the beginning when truck rates were established based on railroad tariffs. One trucking company history includes a poem about the "Rate Clerk's Nightmare" that sums it all up (Broehl 1954:159). Even after a couple of years of study, the logic behind rate-making still eludes me, and I am not alone. Listen to Steve talking about "reefers," or refrigerated trailers:

> The poorest paid trucks on the road today are your reefers, and they're your most expensive. (Why are they poorly paid, Steve?) I have no idea. I tried to figure that out. For twenty-seven years I tried to figure that out. When I started in the reefer business—that was in 1951, September of 1951. After thirty-two months with Northwest Trucking, I got fired for refusing a load out of St. Louis, and I went with another company out of Chicago. That was a perishable haul, but you had to have your own trailer. So I bought my own trailer. And lucky Steve, again he got a lemon. Seems to be my fate.
>
> But anyhow, even then the reefers were underpaid, when you considered the investment and what you've got to put up with. To start off with—especially a railer. Now that name might not mean anything to you. "Railer" is just a shortening of the term "meat railer," which carries the meat suspended from the roof instead of laid on the floor. A meat railer, as a rule, weighs two-three thousand pounds more than an ordinary refrigerated trailer because of the extra supports for holding that meat up. Usually a driver carries a set of hooks with him for hanging the meat on. There's another several hundred pounds. Also, part of his loading space is taken up by the hooks. The trailer has to be washed to put a load on. Then after you haul it naturally there's fat against the wall and blood dripping off the carcass meat. Then you've got to wash it after it gets empty. You'd think for all this you'd get extra compensation. You don't.
>
> (You don't get anything at all?) No. I represent Double M Trucking here. I run the office for them. I can take their tariff book out of that drawer over there and show you where loads out of the West for swinging meat—the hanging meat—or floor loads pay the identical same price. Why, you could put a load of box meat on and never dirty the trailer. All that'd rub the wall would be the box. No fat. No blood.
>
> (There's no logic to that.) There is no logic but that's the way it is. Plus you've got the expense of a unit. You've got to feed it with fuel. You've got to feed it with oil. And it's always breaking a line or something where you've got to feed it with the. . . . Sooner or later you've got to do maintenance on it for refrigeration. You've got the risk of spoilage. You've got the risk of theft, which happened to me here a couple of years ago; three times in less than three months.

A "reefer" looks like a regular van, except for a rectangular box stuck on its front end. In the box is a small diesel and a refrigeration unit. Reefers are necessary, obviously, to keep a load at a certain temperature—warmer or cooler than the ambient temperature. The independent, as usual, is responsible for the load. If it arrives too warm or too cool, the customer can file a claim or even reject it. If that happens, the independent is the proud new owner of forty thousand pounds of warm lettuce.

Reefers cost more than regular vans; the refrigeration unit requires more care; extra weight is involved so the "payload" is less. Given all this, Steve cannot understand why the rates for reefer loads are low. He goes on to give two examples that pay the same. One load, boxed meat, is easier to handle, does not require cleaning, and involves no additional equipment. Swinging meat, on the other hand, requires rails, hooks, and trailer cleaning. The rates are the same. As I say, and as Steve agreeably repeats, there is no logic to that.

Here is another story Steve told about rates, one where I badgered him a bit to try to learn about the ICC's role:

> The carrier submits them to the ICC, and then they are approved and published. The carrier sets these rates, and that's what's going on right now. The carriers are cutting rates. I don't know how they can operate, Mike. Believe me, what they're cutting them to is twenty years ago, and believe me, there's a lot of difference between the costs twenty years ago and today. A lot. I'll give you an example of what I meant about the rates. Back when I first was hauling reefer, which was 1951–52, one of the guys that I used to haul with was hauling radiators for $1.22 a hundred. You could haul those on a flatbed, and if it rained on them it wouldn't mean anything. I was hauling hay which had to be protected for $1.20. [brief exchange omitted]
>
> The strange thing is it seems like the more valuable the cargo is the cheaper the rate. We haul a lot of sugar out of here. The rate on sugar is way down. It's real low. But God help you if you tear a bag, because you'll haul for nothing. Because it's very easy. I had one guy call me up. He had hundred-pound bags on. He must have had forty-two–forty-three thousand pounds so you're talking 430 bag. And he dropped seventeen of them on the way. Seventeen hundred-pound bags. And he got a big problem if it's turned down. At that time sugar was going thirty–thirty-one dollars for a hundred-pound bag, I think. The work probably only paid him four something. He had five hundred dollars right there.

Steve introduces the problem of rate-cutting, saying that rates have come down to "twenty years ago." He once again shows the lack of "rhyme or reason" by comparing the rate for radiators, which can be hauled on a "flatbed" trailer, with that for hay, which has to be protected. Flatbeds, the level platform-type trailers, are less expensive and the freight requires less care. So why was the rate the same?

Steve's assertion that the more valuable freight has cheaper rates goes against the traditional wisdom that higher valued commodities have higher rates, but he gives a specific example. Sugar rates have dropped, but the value of the freight is high. An independent breaks

Independents Declared

17 out of 430 bags; he is liable for $510 worth of damage on a load that paid him "four something." If he has to pay for the broken bags, he ran for fun and not for profit.

Adding to the confusion around rates are the classification systems, categories that cover anything that can be put on a truck. Depending on how the carrier classifies the load it might be in a more or less expensive rate category. One trucking company history describes the problem of whether to call childrens' balloons "rubber balloons" or "toys" (Broehl 1954). The toy category had a higher rate for the freight. In the following segment, Irv responds to my questions on classification:

> (See, I've always wondered if sometimes they don't mess around with that a little bit. Like even take the same freight and if you call it this it's that much.) You can find it two and three-four-five-six different places in the rate book. (Can you? I was wondering about that.) Yes, you can. (I was wondering about that.) Oh was you? You wasn't at the last meeting, was you? (Yeah.) You were. Well, did you hear the woman from the ICC when I asked her about the rates? She said, "Well, you could always look it up." (Oh, yeah.) Yeah. Did you hear that? I told her I didn't have the rest of my life to spend on it.
>
> If you can find one thing listed at a dozen places in the rate books, how do you know which one applies? It's from point A on one hand to point B on the other hand, providing it's so and so. Or point B on one hand to point A on the other hand providing so and so. And 'time you get through with all this damn legal jumble shit you don't know what you're doing. To me if they say raw steel it should be raw steel, period. It don't make a damn whether it runs from point A to point B, or point C to point G. What the hell's the difference? The U.S. government and no other government can't put out anything that isn't so damned complicated it takes a Philadelphia lawyer a year to decipher it. They can't do it. It's impossible.

Independents lived for years with the rates that Steve and Irv describe. They just had to know enough to ask what the rate was and then know how to figure whether the run was profitable. But lately, with the deregulation and recession pressures, the insanity has taken a turn for the worse. Right now The Issue is rate-cutting.

Rate-Cutting

With deregulation comes lower prices; that is, of course, the idea—enable competition and prices will decline. Unfortunately, with the added effect of a recession, the impact on the lone independent with no control over rates becomes the economic equivalent of the rack. In some of the interviews, independents gave specific examples of rate-cutting. Here is an example from Cal:

The rates was more stabilized then. You didn't have all this cut-rating thing. If we got ninety-five cents a hundred we went along hauling for a year. The next year the rate went up a little bit, we got the increase in rate. It seems like each year we were getting a little increase. And everybody's rates was about the same. Today you got a half a dozen different rates running Chicago. And some of them is running—if they think that this is safety. There's no way that you can have safety when you send a truck out of here for $1.71 and $1.70. And now they tell me that this one company's down to $1.50 to Chicago. And you got five hundred dollars left for that truck and that driver to go to Chicago. There's no way that that man can operate a decent piece of equipment and stay in business.

Before he talks about rate-cutting, Cal describes this carrier as good because it had loads or permitted trip-leasing without taking any of the payment. He blames rate-cutting for current problems. In an earlier segment, he elaborated on the connection between rates and safety:

Deregulation—as far as I'm concerned, deregulation isn't the answer to the question. (What do you think is?) Well, deregulation just feeds more to this thing of what I was talking about. Trucks running all over the country. Drivers have got nothing to look forward to, if you go out here and you deregulate freight that every Tom, Dick, and Harry can haul it. I know for an instance—I was down at this place on Fisk Highway, and you talk about cutting rates. They have cut rates something fierce. One company—they'd fight over that freight. One company cuts it and another company cuts it. We were in there one day that a truck was loading for Boston. Both front tires showing the cord. This is your cheap carriers you're getting today. Nonunion outfits. That's all they're worried about is how cheap I can ship it. You got fellows that's cutting the rates so low that there's no way they can operate a decent piece of equipment up and down the road.

Cal's connection of lower rates with safety is made by others, and again in his remark that the companies "figure that if you like to drive truck well enough you'll settle for half." When the independent is not making his operating costs he has to cut corners; when he cuts corners he tries for a little extra on that tire. When that tire is the single one of the steering axle, a blowout almost guarantees an accident. It can be that simple and that dangerous.

Since 1981, I have sat in on Senate and House oversight hearings on the progress of trucking deregulation. Witnesses often distinguish carefully between economic and safety regulation, arguing that the latter must, of course, remain in place. Yet Cal's passage is a reminder that the relationship between the two regulatory domains "on the ground" is far from well understood.

An example from the trucker's eye view will show how low the rates are. Say that the truck is carrying forty-five thousand pounds of freight. (With a thirty-five-thousand-pound empty weight, that puts it at the eighty-thousand-pound legal limit.) At $1.71 per hundred, the total is $769.50. Say the independent gets 75 percent of that, though many carriers are dropping the percentage to 72 percent, as Red points out:

> It's rather interesting that the rate of payment went up to 75 percent and has now gone back down to 72 percent as pretty much of a standard, largely because of the rate-cutting that's come about since the Motor Carrier Reform Act. Carriers claim that that's the only way they can stay in business. They have to get more revenue. And a lot of the special commodities or steel hauler divisions—some of them have been closed down because the companies claim they can't pay the union benefits and all of that. And a lot of them have been restarted as nonunion. And they still only pay the 72 percent, generally speaking. The owner/operator's always been pretty much at the mercy of the carrier.

Staying with the traditional 75 percent in the hypothetical example gives the independent $577, less other "chargebacks" that might be on the settlement sheet. The Rand-McNally U.S. highway map gives 668 miles as the distance from Baltimore to Chicago. At the time of Cal's story, he would have received compensation for fuel (the program has now been overturned in court), which at 13.5 cents per mile gives him $90 more, for a total of $667. The actual mileage will be longer. Adding the accepted industry figure of 6 percent for "circuity"—average expected additional mileage over that given in the Household Mover's Guide—is 668 plus 41, for a total of 709 miles. The 709 does not include deadhead miles—the miles he traveled to get to the loading point before the trip started or the miles traveled after unloading to find the next load.

The standard way of figuring revenue is "cents per mile," although independents often say that others do not have the business sense to evaluate their trips this way. Using cents per mile in the hypothetical example is $667 divided by 709, or 94 cents per mile. At the $1.50 rate that Cal mentions, the figure would drop to 84 cents per mile. At the $1.89 rate that his son receives working for a good carrier, the figure rises to 103 cents per mile.

How many cents per mile is enough? Good question. Everybody has a number but it is not always clear what the number includes. Some say that a clear one dollar per mile is the minimum rate to survive as an independent (Will, for example), but most independents say a dollar is too low. In April of 1982 the state of California estimated $1.15. In August of 1982 an independent organization threatened to shut down unless its members got $1.20. In March of 1983 a group of independents decided on $1.40. But for now, the dollar-per-mile figure will be used, even though it may be inadequate. Only the highest rate that Cal quotes meets that goal. Independents everywhere complain about rate-cutting, complain until they go out of business, that is. In their leased-on roles, they have no control over rates; all they can do is refuse to haul the freight.

LTLs

There *is* one way to get better rates. Most independents, when they get a load, put on a trailerful of freight going from one shipper to one customer. That kind of shipment is charged the "truckload" or "TL" rate. The following passage is from Cal again, describing a "less than truckload" (LTL) rate as he goes through his records and looks at trips recently run by his son:

> Now, my average stuff going Chicago—I keep a book here. That's a load of junk. This happens once in a while when you get a chance to come out when you're running with a good company, and a company that's got good freight. Now, this is one of our own companies that the truck is leased to. There's $963 left in the truck but the boy he's got four drops on it. He's on that run right now. He'll be three days getting that freight off. He didn't used to have to do that. He'll well earn his money.
>
> (Is that to Chicago also?) That's a Chicago load. (Why is the rate so good on that one? Is it the kind of stuff he's hauling?) Well, he's got all LTL freight on it. He's got four LTLs on. (And the rates are higher for LTLs.) And the rates are higher for LTLs. That only happens once in a great while.

Although it will take additional time to get the load off, there's $936 left "in the truck"—that is, left over after the driver's wage has been deducted.

The secret is that Cal's son has "LTLs" on—"less than truckload" shipments. Shippers pay proportionately more for an LTL because several LTLs have to be consolidated and put on a single truck, then broken up and delivered at the destinations. LTL freight is the source of profit for most of the major carriers; seldom does an independent see any of it. Dave also describes an LTL load:

> You know, ever since I been out and just going in—like before when I was up there in my company truck, I'd go into Chicago and they'd give me a little bitty bit of nothing, you know. "Hey, you got any LTLs to stick on?" "Any what's? Never heard of them." I went up there week before last, I guess now. Took me two days to load it. I loaded a twenty-three thousand pound . . . and three LTLs. Fourteen hundred dollars for a load.

Dave, the independent who wandered in during Steve's interview, had been leased to a carrier. Recently he threw it over to become a gypsy. The irony of his story is that as a gypsy he went back to his carrier and got the higher paying LTLs. Since he does not say where the load was going, the cents per mile cannot be computed, but the $1,400 figure and the context of the story suggest that he has done very well. LTLs provide one way to make money, even in a time of rate-cutting.

Rate Tricks

The pressure on carriers due to deregulation and recession leads to a particular kind of "carrier trick" described more fully in chapter 6. The carrier quotes the independent one rate and then pays him another. Terry, a Baltimore independent, showed me one such case. ABC quoted him a rate, but after he finished the trip they paid him another rate that was about twenty cents per hundred weight cheaper. He complained to ABC, but ABC claimed the original rate was a mistake. Terry's wife, who like most, takes care of the books, went to work calling the ICC. An agency official known for his sympathy to independents looked into Terry's problem and called with apologies to say he could do nothing. Terry's only recourse was to go after the carrier (whose offices were in another state) with a civil suit. The time and expense involved in such a suit led Terry and his wife to give up the case as a lost cause.

Though not standard practice, carriers employ another rate trick called "flat-rating," which is perfectly legal as long as the lease describes it. A carrier offers an independent a flat fee for hauling the load rather than a percentage of the actual rate. Since the flat fee is typically less than the seventy-some percent an independent usually gets, the carrier can retain more of the revenue, obviously at the independent's expense. Once again, flat-rating is encouraged by the current economic pressure on carriers. Will talked about it in his interview.

> See, and then I noticed another thing too. Ray Express started something new with their brokers. They have little agencies. What they do, their home base is in North Carolina. And now they have a little office here in Baltimore, which just makes phone calls and gets loads. And when they don't have their company drivers they trip-lease them, when they get 25-30 percent. I think they pay 72 percent when they trip-lease. I also found out in order to stimulate freight or stimulate their agents to get more freight, if they could trip-lease a load and flat rate it—say if the load paid nine hundred dollars and they could find a guy sitting around that's been sitting—they know people are sitting around. If they could find a guy to haul that load,

and say it's going back to where he lives, he'll take it for fuel money. Let's say five or six hundred dollars on a nine-hundred-dollar load. If they can flat rate it to a guy, the agents get 30 percent. So that's like a bonus incentive for them. But what's that going to do for the company drivers? If they think they can find some jerk that'll take it for five hundred why would they even give it to a company driver and have to pay where the main office gets all the money, you know. [example omitted]

And guys will do it. You know, if you're sitting in Florida and you want to go home, or you can't get a load going back towards where you live, and you know it costs you three hundred dollars for fuel, wouldn't you take a load for four hundred and figure, well, I'm making a hundred dollars and I'm on my way home? That's the whole thing. So they do it. (Is that pretty standard, Will, in the industry?) No, far as I know that just started with them about three months ago, you know. But for some reason—hey, you know, if you're in business you look around and you say how can I make more money. You go up at the truck stop, there's a hundred trucks sitting there. You know, a guy wants to go home and he don't really want to go home empty. It's not that much trouble to throw four hundred dollars on there and the other guy gets five.

A carrier gives its agents incentive to flat rate a load by offering them a share of the difference between the percentage and the flat rate. Add some independents sitting around trying to get a load who live where the freight is going. Presto—the carrier gets more than expected and the independent settles for less to get out of whatever he is and head home.

Little wonder that when I first started using the term "backhaul" I sometimes got a stern look and a quick "there is no such thing as a backhaul." A backhaul, as the term suggests, is a load you take to get "back" home. For an independent, there are no backhauls; there are just loads. When he runs cheap he is not making any money. It is obvious that for most shipments from point A to point B, there will be some trucks around A that want to go home to B. The idea of a "backhaul" threatens to lower rates even more, to the carrier's advantage and the independent's detriment. Will again:

It's like a lot of times I'm sitting around these offices. When I was working for Ray, and he had guys calling in, and they say, you know—the guy might have a load going to Kansas but this guy wants to go to Florida. Or he wanted to come back over on the East Coast someplace. Or it was out West. And the guy might want to come back this way, so he's not going to take that load. But if a guy lives in Kansas, and the shipper's paying the company nine hundred or a thousand dollars to haul that load, say, "Hey, yeah, I got a load for you going right past your house." The first thing they ask is where you live, you know. And that way they figure, well if they can send you back past your house they can probably get you to haul it at a cheaper rate.

The threat of running empty—deadheading—appears again. When the truck is empty the independent is not making money, and unfortunately, everybody in the trucking world knows that and uses it to get him to run cheap. Ike sums up the whole economic squeeze with rate-cutting as the centerpiece:

> (Ike, if a young guy came up to you and asked you for advice—he was thinking of being an owner/operator. He was going to go into business maybe. What would you tell him? What would be the most important thing?) I would tell him not right now. Now is not the time. Number one is this. With the Reagan administration and with the Nixon administration, with the fuel and with the price of equipment, you can't make it. Number one, you get a decent truck, it's going to cost you too much. You got the same freight rate running right today as it was back in 1967, '68, '69, and '70, and some cases it's running cheaper. So he can't make it any way because he don't know. If he gets out there and he goes to try to start trucking and he goes on the scales—the first time he get on the scales and the man look out there and see him, if he have problems the first thing he going to do, he going to come out there and they going to fine him if he don't know how to get around the scales. And yet and still, you can't go legal. If you go legal, you ain't going to make it, because you can't haul legal freight and expect to make money, because it's impossible.

Ike summarizes the general problem of declining rates after the inflationary 1970s. His philosophy is that the only way to make money is to run heavy and hot. In this passage, he draws from that assumption and talks about how making it depends on knowing how to get around the scales.

Economic conditions were grim during the study period, forcing many independent truckers out of business. In their third year follow-up of the ICC survey sample, Corsi, Gardner, and Tuck (1982:7) reported that half of the original sample were no longer leased to a carrier. Of the half that had left, about 40 percent were out of trucking altogether, about 25 percent were driving company trucks, and about 15 percent had gone into exempt hauling.

Of course not only the independents are going out of business; the trade magazines, and some of the interviews, are filled with reports of the turmoil of the deregulated recessionary marketplace. No one in the industry yet knows what will happen. Deregulation is working in the sense that competition has increased and rates for service have dropped. But leased independents have no control over pricing or inflation. It does not take an accountant to notice the changes, as Jack points out:

(Jack, what's an example of how the rates have been cut? Can you give me an example?) Alright, see, that's something I can't do, Mike, because I never pay that much attention to what I'm making. My wife handles all of that. See, hey, a business man I'm not. You know that. I mean, I know that I can't make it now. That's all I know. When it comes to, you know, business and stuff, I don't know that much about it, because my wife handles all of that. I'll put it this way. I could go out and go to Boston, and I could take a hundred dollars and go to Boston and come back. And I could pay tolls going up and buy fuel going up and coming back. And I'd still have twenty-thirty dollars left in my pocket when I got home here. Hey, to go to Boston now, I got to take something like 350 dollars one way. To get up there one way, you know. I mean this is how I see it. I see it on my advances and stuff like this, you know, what I got to pay when I'm out on the highway. This is where I see it, you know. And I can go in and buy breakfast, and Jesus Christ, you're talking four to five dollars for a lousy stinking breakfast. And I mean, it's a lousy stinking breakfast is what it is. It's nothing. And you're still hungry when you walk away from the place.

No wonder that Ike sums up his overview of independent trucking with:

With the price of the fuel it is today, and with the deregulation, you're going to have to be a good one to stay in business.

That, of course, is just what deregulation is supposed to do; reward the competent, bring the efficient to the top. The problem for leased independents is that they can only watch costs increase while revenues decline. There is nothing they can do about it. They have no control over rates.

Chapter 6

Carrier Tricks

Messing with Your Money

Some time after a trip ends, an independent submits paperwork to a carrier; some days later, he receives a check and a "settlement sheet." The sheet shows a list of payments and charges, with the net pay at the bottom. Paper (signed freight bills, fuel receipts, logbooks) in; money (minus travel advances, worker's compensation, permit costs) out. Since the carrier controls this transformation from paper to money, it is no surprise that the independent worries about "carrier tricks"—the different ways that unethical carriers manage to get more of his money than they should.

In some cases, the carrier can just cheat. Honest mistakes, of course, do happen, but some accounts, like this one from Irv, show outright dishonesty.

> I stayed with AB Freight I guess about three years. I got tired of calling every week to tell them my pay was wrong. Everybody claims— and it almost has to be a fact—that AB sends their employees that worked in the payroll department to school. If you don't learn to cheat, you don't work for them. Hey, how else can a man pay you fifty-two times and make fifty-two mistakes in his favor? (They were all in their favor?) Always. Always. And never a mistake in your favor. Never.
>
> I've already got paid from AB on the same identical load three different times and got three different rates. (On the same load?) Same identical load, from the same point to the same point. (Using the same classification?) Same classifi—well, what classification they put it in I don't know, but it's the same identical freight.

Later in the same interview, Irv tells a story about Ike, who became so annoyed with AB's cheating that he finally brought on a confrontation.

In his own interview, Ike talked about a subtler type of trick. If an independent delivers the freight late or in damaged condition, the shipper can file a *claim* against the carrier for whom he works. According to Ike, it is possible for a claim to be manufactured:

> (How long were you with Colonial?) I stayed with them about eighteen months. (Huh, what made you decide to change?) Because Colonial started taking my money. They claimed that I had a claim of nine hundred dollars. And I went up to . . . I was hauling regular out of there, and they had to write a letter and all of that and tell them that they didn't put no claim in to it. So I asked Tommy, "Tommy, why you take my money?" He said, "Well, Ike," he said, "we got to reach from somewhere and take some money from somebody. So we drawed your name out of the hat and so we thought we could get away with yours. But we give you your money back." So it took me about six months to get my nine hundred dollars back, and I told them, well, I think it was about time for me to go, and I left.
>
> I went and bought my own trailer and then I went to Midstate. Then Midstate pulled my lease in 1980. (They said you were making too much money.) I was making too much money. So I left them and I been back out on my own. And I don't think I ever lease no more to another company. In fact I know I won't. They hire people to take from me, to steal from me any way they can get some money to stay in business. So I ain't no slave and I'm not going to lease on to them no more. So that's it.

Colonial told Ike it had a claim against him. Claims come in a variety of forms (an actual case is presented in chapter 10). For example, a produce customer might file a claim if the load arrived so late that he "missed a market." Or another customer might claim that the temperature in a refrigerated trailer was too low or too high. A "dry freight" customer might complain if the load had shifted around during the trip, causing some damage. Legitimate claims often occur. But after his story of the fake claim, Ike concludes with the general assertion that he will not lease to a carrier again because "they all steal from you."

In other segments, Ike talks about another carrier trick. When an independent leases on, he is usually required to put up an escrow deposit with the carrier. As Ike tells it, a carrier wanted him to deadhead several hundred miles to pick up a cheap load for a short run; when he refused, the carrier fired him and kept his four hundred dollars escrow money. Will tells a similar story about lost escrow, involving fifteen hundred dollars held by two different carriers. The ICC survey also reports problems with escrow accounts. One fourth

Independents Declared

of the sample had not received *any* escrow money when they left and said they did not expect to see it. Of those who did get it back (some waiting several months), about 40 percent said that the carriers had made deductions.

Fake claims and lost escrow problems occur, but infrequently. More common are disputes over the settlement sheet and the documentation of charges and payments for each trip. Before detailing some of them, consider one example of an independent's theory—this one is Red's—of how incentives to try the tricks are built into the system:

> CTP several years later became union, but at the time I went to work for them it was nonunion. But it was still a pretty decent place to work, as long as you kept close tabs on your settlement sheets, because the vice-president of CTP Freight Lines that ran the division was on a commission basis, or on a bonus system based on his net profit. And his wife was the chief bookkeeper for the division. So it was pretty hard—whenever you had any questions, why it was pretty hard to come up with some answers sometimes. But all in all it was—thanks mainly to Vance, Baltimore terminal manager, it was a pretty decent place to work.

According to Red, the more the man in charge cheated in favor of the company, the higher the company share of the revenue, and the greater his bonus. If an independent called CTP to question any of the payments or charges, he talked to the man's wife, hardly a disinterested party.

Stories of settlement sheet tricks are scattered throughout the interviews. Will tells a story about the now extinct "surcharge," the fuel supplement based on a percentage of the rate:

> Now, what else happened was the competition amongst carriers hauling containers. There doesn't seem to be any regulation. If there is I don't know about it. Regulation on rates. And they come in and cut rates like it's unreal. And what finally got me disgusted was we were hauling say a set of chassis from Baltimore to Jersey, and they were paying two hundred dollars. They'd pay two hundred dollars. We were on a flat rate, but they still broke it down with the surcharge. It was two hundred fifty plus the surcharge which came up to about seventy-two dollars, which apparently they were charging two hundred up and thirty-six dollar surcharge. I think it was 18 percent then. O.K. And then the same thing coming back on the other end. So that gave them four hundred. Yeah, right. We got two hundred fifty plus the surcharge which was seventy-two dollars.
>
> They lost the freight from this one outfit due to a billing error. These people were Steamship Lines. They're particular about billing, and the office somehow made a mistake and they lost them as a cus-

tomer. So over a period of time they were trying to get them back. So what they did, they cut the rate again. Said, "Well, we'll haul the chassis up there for two hundred dollars, but you don't have to pay the surcharge." That's great. The customer never did have to pay the surcharge according to Interstate Commerce Commission, but the carrier did. And the carrier didn't call us in and ask us, "Hey, how about splitting it? We'll make it like they'll pay half the surcharge and take . . ."—even if they'd have took the thirty-six dollars off the two hundred dollars and still gave us the surcharge it would have looked good. But when they take it away, and you know they're doing it illegally. They took the surcharge away from the drivers. They only gave us a flat two hundred fifty, see.

So anyway, rather than get involved in that again I said, well, I let them go three trips, and then they made a mistake and overpaid me a hundred dollars. I said—well I'd run three trips like that, so it was 90 dollars plus 18 is 108 dollars. I got a hundred of it back on another mistake that they made, and rather than go through—like I said I don't want to be a damn crusader against every company. And it would be every company because none of them comply.

To understand Will's story requires some background. He was hauling "containers," metal boxes, twenty or forty feet long, that are stacked on oceangoing freighters. The advantage to using containers is that they can be taken off the ship, lowered onto a trailer chassis, and hooked onto a tractor. If a ship docks in the Baltimore harbor with containers for Philadelphia, the Philadelphia containers are offloaded onto trucks and sent on their way.

Will describes how the rate for containers (a full one up and an empty one back) brings the carrier four hundred dollars. Rather than getting a percentage, independents were paid a flat rate of two hundred fifty dollars for the trip up and back—the "round." At the time of Will's story, the fuel supplement was based on a percentage of the gross—18 percent was the figure, for a grand total of seventy-two dollars on the four hundred dollars.

After it lost Steamship's business, the company decided to drop the rate to lure it back. But rather than cutting the actual rate, it just stopped charging the shipper for the surcharge and then stopped paying it to the independents. Will suggests that if the company had called the independents in and talked about it, the independents might have been willing to make some concessions to get the business because the recession had started and freight was drying up. But instead, the company just stopped paying it. Will "got it back another way" by taking advantage of a settlement sheet error in his favor, using an "independent trick" to cancel out the carrier's trick. He closes with the now familiar refrain that the specific story he tells is typical—they all steal from you. In this case, an ICC-mandated

Independents Declared

program that resulted from the shutdown was converted into another carrier trick.

Fuel Taxes

Another carrier trick is an elaborate ruse to get some of the fuel tax money required by the permit system used in most states. When freight moves interstate, the truck must have *fuel permits*, the multicolored stickers displayed on one side or the other of the tractor. States require fuel permits so that they get a share of the state tax added on to the price of diesel fuel.

The fuel tax is best explained by an example. Suppose that Red is making a roundtrip from Baltimore to New York City. He carries two hundred gallons of fuel, which at four to five miles a gallon will take him eight hundred to a thousand miles, more than enough to make the round. Imagine that there is a small fuel stop in Maryland that has bargain prices on diesel, and that Maryland has a lower tax per gallon than the other states along the way. It makes sense for Red to fuel up there all the time. But then he would never buy fuel in any other state, and those other states will get none of the tax that is added on at their fuel pumps. Fuel permits are a response to this situation.

When an independent finishes his trip, he turns in receipts for all the fuel he has purchased. The carrier calculates miles run and fuel purchased. If the independent did not purchase enough to cover the tax for the miles run, the carrier may deduct for the missing tax on his settlement sheet. But what if he buys too much fuel?

I got to be good friends with the fuel tax man down there. And we used to go down and visit him and his wife, stay overnight at their house once in a while. And one time I asked him what happens to the money that the company collects that they don't have to use to send to these states. And he said, "I wish you hadn't asked me that question, because I can't answer it." He said, "I can answer it, but I can't answer it." I said, "I got you." (That was the answer.) That was the answer.

Not too long after that he was fired. I felt very sorry for him, because he did a good job, and he really didn't have a whole lot to say about it. The man had no legs. Both legs were amputated right below the hip, and his potential for employment was now limited. And those buggers fired him. I guess he—I didn't do it. Maybe he made the mistake of confiding in somebody else that the company found out. But anyhow, they canned him. I don't know how much money they made that way, just by keeping fuel taxes that they didn't have to report. Then later on I found out that a couple of the other carriers that I was leased to weren't reporting all the miles that we ran in those states anyhow. So they were pocketing even the legitimate fuel tax—a portion of it. And I wouldn't be at all surprised but what this company was doing the same thing.

Red keeps all his fuel receipts plus a record of all the miles he runs in each state. At the end of his trip, he submits these records to the carrier to do the paperwork. If Red does not buy enough fuel in New Jersey to pay the tax he would have paid at New Jersey pumps, he will find on his settlement sheet a deduction for the amount of fuel tax owed.

Red's story shows how the carrier manages a fleet. By billing independents for unpaid tax, the carrier never has to pay it. But if the fleet buys *more* fuel than is necessary to pay the tax for miles run, it results in an overpayment to a particular state, and the carrier can apply for a refund. Over time, a carrier can accumulate a surplus of fuel tax paid. According to Red, when the money came back, refunds were never returned to the independents.

The following account from Will describes a change in Maryland regulations that addresses fuel tax inequities:

O.K., so then I found out about a company. I went to work for Bowline out of Connecticut, hauling trailers off the rail system out of Alexandria, Virginia. That was a good company to work for. They complied with all the regulations to a certain degree. I'd say they were probably about 80 percent in compliance. But then you got a disadvantage with them. They're out of Connecticut, and I wound up getting paid on Mondays, which made life tough when you're used to getting paid on a Friday. They used computers, and they kept a running tab on your state mileage, on your fuel tickets—your fuel permit. And it wound up that they were nailing you. Like I was running from Baltimore to Boston area and back again, and you can't buy fuel in every state. I mean you probably could, but it would be a pain in the butt, because from here to Boston is only four hundred miles. And if you fill your tank up once you'd have to buy like twenty dollars-thirty dollars worth of fuel in each state. But anyway, they took a running tab of that, and every trip they were nailing you for two or three dollars off of this trip for fuel tax. [description of workman's compensation omitted]

So you know, you sit down, you say, "Well, jeez, I made two thousand dollars this week. I ought to clear after my expenses a thousand." Then you look and then they got the road tax taken out. Then they take workman's comp out. Majority of the companies don't do it the way Bowline does. The majority of the companies figure that if I don't buy fuel in one state, somebody else will. I've never looked into how companies pay the fuel tax. Whether they pay it on each individual driver or if they pay on so many permits that they have whomever they're issued to. But they're all in that company's name. The only difference on the fuel ticket would be that

Independents Declared

East Coast. And we got all their junk trailers and all that. And most of the money that, you know, we used for expenses on LKW's trailers all had to go on these other trailers to get them up to date so we could pull them in California. And it's just a big hassle with them. It was actually more or less a little war between the East Coast drivers and the West Coast drivers. A West Coast driver'd go out east. They'd let him sit there and sit there and sit there. They wouldn't really give him a load. They'd always load the Mesa trucks first around the LKW. And then you get out west here the same thing. Mesa trucks'd sit and the LKW trucks'd go.

But they just started going downhill. The money started getting tighter. Until they merged with Mesa, we never had to wait for our money. We always got paid. And then when they started merging with Mesa, our money was up to six weeks behind. (Six weeks?) Six-eight weeks behind, yeah. I hauled a load that I run for this mining company that I haul loads for now. I hauled a load for them and I run it through the company. And they sent the bill to the mining company. He paid it. And it was seven weeks later I finally got my money.

While Dan teaches us about an expensive carrier trick—forcing independents to buy company-owned trailers, he repeats some of the topics encountered earlier. He also speaks of the carrier's deteriorating personal tone, a topic explored more fully in the next chapter.

Over and over again in this chapter independents say that carriers cheat, either directly, or by holding back escrow money or requiring equipment purchases, or by manipulating charges that show up on the settlement sheet. Earlier the teachers described rate tricks like quoting one and paying another. These stories occur so often, in taped interviews, informal conversations, and official meetings, that one begins to agree with the many strong assertions that "they're all like that." But such a conclusion ignores the admittedly rarer favorable descriptions already quoted and others to come. On trips and in conversations independents sometimes single out a carrier as good to work for. And it is not unusual for an independent to stay with a carrier for several years.

But, generally, independents describe carriers as greedy and untrustworthy. Carriers control the transformation of paperwork to paycheck, and in the details of that transformation lies plenty of room to maneuver money around to its own advantage. By the interview accounts, the profit motive of the carriers and their agents does not guarantee anything but the relevance of the maxim—"Let the independent beware." Carl summed up his time-tested strategy this way:

If I didn't trust the carrier, I wired for two advances on the way, you know. And I'd leave him holding about fifty bucks. If I didn't get that, shame on them. You got to know who to haul for and who not to haul for.

Even if the independent is experienced and knowledgeable about companies and personnel, as Carl is, he is still a potential victim of carrier tricks. The only recourse is to "get it back another way," using a trick like Will's failure to report carrier overpayments, or others recounted in the following chapters. But in the game of tricks, the cards are stacked in favor of the carrier.

Since the carriers control the paycheck, the prices, and the access to the freight, the independent must lease on with caution. Two other characteristics of carriers came up repeatedly in the interviews, characteristics that are important in guiding the independent's choice. First, if the carrier has all the power and the ICC cannot realistically do much to help, what about the union? Second, what about that elusive but important personal "feel" of the place?

Chapter 7

The Carrier Setting

Unions

Independents depend on carriers for freight, rates, and payments. The tone of dependence and powerlessness expressed in the interviews suggests that they have the kind of problems that unions were designed to solve. But the Teamsters are hardly the paragon, and the relationship between independents and the Teamsters has been difficult, since independents threaten their control of the availability of trucks and drivers. (See Maister 1980:133ff. for a sketch of their mutual history.)

The union is not often discussed in the interviews; when it does come up, the remarks tend to be unfavorable. Most independents are not enthusiastic about unions, to put it mildly. They are independent contractors rather than employees and unions are for employees. In the ICC survey, 22 percent of leased independents claimed union membership; the survey did not ask how many of that 22 percent were forced to join.

On the one hand, the independent might have to join because he has leased on with an otherwise union carrier. The union allows leasing independents to carry the low-rated truckload freight that the company could not afford to carry in its own trucks with Teamster drivers. In return, the independents have to become union members. But there may be other reasons as well, as Red explains.

> The first one was a union job that I never did see a union card. 'Course I was only there for six weeks. But they had us enrolled in some local in Maryland that nobody ever heard of. I don't know that they had any membership except the people in this company. And I don't know of anybody that ever filed a grievance, or if they did ever

had one processed. I mean, it was strictly a sweetheart deal to enable the carrier to deliver anywhere. You know, if you go on into a place, say a construction job or something like that, or some of these steel mills where they have real tight unions, sometimes a shop steward will come over, ask a truck driver that's delivering there or picking up there to see his union card. So if you didn't have one, some of these places, they'd refuse to handle your freight. I don't know—that isn't what they call a secondary boycott, is it? I don't know. But anyhow, that's the way it would be sometimes. In some places, not too awful many. But they had us in the union just in case that ever happened.

Red describes the union as only a hedge against possible problems in loading or unloading. In his view, the union was a necessary evil, a required membership that only allowed him to work and provided nothing in return.

Red's statement is typical of the critical attitude about the Teamsters expressed in the interviews. For example, when I asked Carl why he left one carrier (where he was a company driver) for another, he explained it this way:

Well, the milk company that I was working for went union. And I worked there about a year when they first started with the union. They hired mostly new drivers, and the new drivers wanted a union. I was happy, you know, because we were getting pretty well union scale. The only thing we didn't have was the benefits. But you know, like I said you could leave Sunday and be there Wednesday. Didn't make any difference. So when they first went union, the old man was dead against it. He was going to close up. He wasn't going to have no unions. And it went on I guess about a year. And we were to get like a dollar raise on every run that we run from the time the union started till the time it officially got in, which would have been a considerable amount of money figuring sometimes you make seven runs a week sometimes. Maybe twelve, you know. We had a lot of short runs.

One day I come in to get the truck, and there was a note on the windshield. "Come in the office." I went in the office, and they said, "You're fired." I said, "What do you mean, I'm fired? Been here six years," you know. "What did I do to get fired?" "The governor's broke on the truck." They were all gas trucks you know. The governor was broke. The governor governs the speed. I know I didn't break it. But they come out and picked up the hood, and sure enough the seal was broke on the governor. And the next thing you know, one of the other drivers run a couple of hours late. They fired him. So what they were doing, they were getting ready to sign up for the union. And all the old guys that's been there so long had all this retroactive pay coming, and they didn't want to pay it, so they must have made a deal with the union. You know, I didn't care if they fired me. I just

Independents Declared

turn around and get my pay. When I went down to the union, they said, "Pay ain't retroactive, because you don't work here no more." You know, getting screwed, that's all. So they fired all the old guys, kept the young guys, didn't have to pay all that money. The union got in. You know that's the trouble with the union. If they couldn't get in—it looked like it was tough—then they'd make a deal . . . of the employer. What the hell. Who cares about the employee? Especially in them days, you could hire all the help you wanted.

By Carl's account, not only was the union no help; he lost his job as a consequence of the sweetheart contract they negotiated to get into the company. Another story, from Will's interview, also argues that unions worry more about relationships with carriers than they do about drivers:

It was a union job. And what was happening, we were having a fight with the union, because the union more or less sided with the company. So we had problems with the union. Well, we still had problems with the company. If you have a hearing before the union committees—I guess you know how they work. It's two people from the company and two people from the union. And nine times out of ten, if the union sides with you the company'll side against you. So that deadlocks it. And then you got to go to another arbitrator. Then they got into the habit of—say, if they want to get rid of one guy, they fire ten guys, and let nine of them come back, but keep the one that they didn't want off.

So there was really no way to win without becoming—I don't know what you would call it. A crusader is really what you'd have to be. And then you probably wouldn't win anyway, you know. And eventually, in the long run, everybody that ever crusaded against the union and the company always got knocked down one way or another. We had a guy that was a real fighter, and he got to be president of the local union. And everybody was gung ho. And when he got too hot on the company the international threatened him. And things like that happen, you know. Anyway, I just got tired of it.

By now the union looks like part of the problem rather than part of the solution. Even when there is some pro-union content in the story, the overall tone often becomes ambivalent. For example, Jack tells a long, involved story from his days as a company driver that shows the union in both a favorable and unfavorable light. A specific union official aggressively came to his aid and later provided accurate documentation of his intervention. But the moral of that same story is that neither the union nor the regulatory agencies will protect you. Will also tells a long story, part of which describes the ineffectiveness of the union when he needed its help.

In other discussions in the interviews the negative tone continues, but shifts from "union" to "union driver." An example from Steve's interview:

> They were not union with the owner/operators, but they had union city men in about three different terminals. And when they went to company trucks, they had to be union, and those guys broke it off in them unmercifully on layover time and running out of hours in the logbook. They had guys there that were professionals at running out of hours out in the middle of somewhere where they'd get paid for a motel, get paid for laying out, for not being in a terminal. Breakdowns. I wasn't constructed that way. Even for the money I couldn't do that. I can't see taking advantage of another person's misfortune.

The independents tell a lot of stories about how union drivers are schemers, using regulations to work less and get paid more. Ike suggests that the logbook regulations came about because the union wanted to reduce hours of work. In conversation Dan described several company driver techniques for manufacturing a minor breakdown when they needed one. But the image is obviously a stereotype; most union truckers are not scheming shirkers. Steve's comments suggest a reason for the independents' negative attitudes about union drivers:

> Yeah, well, I have always felt that the union drivers go out there, they don't have a thing to wear out except the seat of their pants. And they are paid a decent wage. Matter of fact, they're paid an exceptionally good wage. These same companies that employ those union drivers that are buying the tractor, buying the trailer, buying the license plate, the fuel, the tires, and everything, will trip-lease an owner/operator and pay him for taking that load through where he provides everything. And he has got to dip into his driver's pay in order to make expenses. And I could never see where that was right. That man is every bit as entitled to the same wage for running that same business as that union driver. He's entitled to a hell of a lot more for the use of his equipment for that time.

True enough. If a person just wants to *drive* a truck, he is better off hiring on as a company employee, even though the truck will be less personalized than one he would buy himself. He will get his wages, and all he needs if he has a problem is the price of a phone call. If he becomes an owner/operator, he gets to have his own truck in return for taking on all the costs of purchase, insurance, and maintenance.

I talked to one former independent at a truck stop. As we talked he leaned against a new Kenworth company-owned tractor that pulled a reefer full of cheese from an agricultural co-op. Why did he make the shift to company employee? "Wanted my weekends back," came the reply. No more weekends working on the truck; no more weekend layovers in distant places waiting for a load; no more weekends trying to make a Monday morning delivery after a delay, courtesy of a winter storm. Although he was not a union member, he was a *company* driver. Independents often use the two terms synonymously. Historically, company drivers were usually also Teamsters. Since deregulation, this is less frequently the case. Even though he is nonunion, this former independent's comments reveal one man's relief at driving a truck he does not need to worry about.

More often than not, the union appears in the interviews as just another institution of no help—even possible harm—to independents. But there are some striking exceptions, exceptions that show that the union is a lifesaver, or at least a powerful ally. The most positive comments came from Cal. At one point in his interview, he described his conversion to a pro-Teamster stance:

> At one time, when I used to run out of Florida, I used to trip-lease all over the country, and I couldn't see this union thing either. Because when you'd go into a town you had to have a union card to unload. It seemed like the Teamsters told you what to do. And I was just like a lot more guys that you got today. I couldn't see it. But after I worked for them a while and worked under the contract for a while and really needed the help that I got, then I could understand what it meant to a family. Because it wasn't only for me, it was for my children and it was for my wife, which to this day they still pay all her medicine and everything. And I just can't see myself how a family can afford to go without some kind of health protection. Because like I said, if it wasn't for the Teamsters today I wouldn't have the home I live in. I wouldn't have the car I got. Because my doctor bills run into thousands and thousands of dollars.

> (And if you leased to a carrier, they don't provide you with those kind of benefits, is that right?) You have nonunion carriers running, like Smith, and they don't give the guys no protection at all. They don't draw no more money. They're still working for a percentage. Some of them's working for a less percentage than the union company's pay. But they get the most of the work because they're a nonunion carrier. They go in and they cut the rates. They cut the rates considerable. They can afford to haul for less because they don't have this welfare to pay to the union, like your health and welfare and your pension plan. Therefore, they can go in and cut the rates. This is what is giving the union companies today a hard way to go. And I'll admit there's a lot of fellows that don't believe in the union. But then you got a lot of fellows that after they have been in it and found out what it means to them, why you couldn't change their mind. And I'm one of those fellows, too, because there was a time you couldn't talk union to me.

Cal has had medical problems all his life. When aging aggravated the problems, his union benefits prevented his financial collapse. Little wonder that he emphasizes the health and welfare benefits aspects of union membership here and elsewhere. In addition to those benefits, Cal also favorably describes his role as shop steward—he played fair, was respected by management, and did some good for other drivers. As he summarized when explaining why he stayed with the union carrier for a long time, "I had everything just the same as a company driver."

Cal was not the only interviewee with good things to say about union carriers. Red, for instance, described one of his leases like this:

> Now, that was a union carrier, and it was a good thing. My earlier days of trucking up until this present job, that was the best job I ever had. They furnished the regular union health and welfare benefits and paid all our fuel and highway taxes. It was a pretty good thing and they were honest people, generally speaking. We had very little trouble with them. And any problems we had were usually a misunderstanding or a simple error and were straightened out. They kept me fairly busy. I made money with them.

Red is talking about a unionized carrier here, not the union itself, but the point comes across. Like Cal, Red mentions the benefits package, but he also brings up some of the other advantages. A union carrier is supposed to absorb some of the independents' operating costs, like fuel and highway taxes. The Teamster-negotiated "National Master Freight Agreement" (Maister 1980:157ff.) contains an impressive list of items for carriers to pay:

> road or mile tax, Social Security tax, compensation insurance, public liability and property damage insurance, bridge tolls, fees for certificates, permits and travel orders, fines and penalties for inadequate certificates, license fees, weight tax and wheel tax, and for loss of driving time due to waiting at state lines, and also cargo insurance (Maister 1980:158, quoting Article 22, section 10 of the 1979–82 Teamster National Master Freight Agreement).

Those are items that the independent usually covers in a nonunion situation. I did not research how well this all works out in practice, but payment of these costs by the carrier would obviously contribute to an independent's profitability.

The general attitude toward the Teamsters is ambivalence. In his study of the Teamsters, Brill (1978) devoted a chapter to a conversation with a Teamster driver in which a similar ambivalence was expressed. In fact, the entire history of Teamsters and owner/operators is a love-hate relationship, love because the union wants to bring them into the organization, hate because independents are a competitive threat to Teamster control of trucking. In the current era of deregulation, some carriers have in fact shifted to leased trucks to reduce their Teamster fleets. And finally, ambivalence is what I used to hear from drivers years ago when I dispatched union trucks in California. In the interviews the prevailing winds are negative. But independents acknowledge that the union does guarantee a health and welfare benefits package, and union carriers pay operating costs that an independent ordinarily has to provide himself.

But in addressing the problems of dependency, unions are not much help. As a representative of independent trucker interests in the day-to-day problems of dealing with carriers, the union is described as ineffective; in some cases, it is part of the problem.

Personalism

If neither the union nor the ICC can help him, what choice does an independent have? He can investigate the personal tone of a carrier, its style and attitudes and its general way of doing business. Consider two contrasting examples from Will's interview. In one of his stories, Will mentioned a dispatcher that he believed "in his heart" was waiting for a payoff to give independents better loads. In another, he talked about a carrier's "family" atmosphere as a reason he wanted employment there. Like Will, many independents talk about the kind of people who work at the carriers as something that can make a difference. Dan described one carrier supervisor in the following passage:

> Yeah, well, they were a good outfit. You never had to worry about your money. You always had it. When I first went to work for them in '74, if you were laid over the weekend in Utah, the boss would take us down to one of the fancier hotels there, and we'd have a steak breakfast. And it'd be more or less a bitch conference. You had any bitches about the company, then you just stood right up and you told the man, you know. That's one thing that I really enjoyed about that company was that every Saturday morning if you were there he'd come to the yard and pick you up. You'd go over there to the Hotel Utah, or some big fancy hotel had a big diningroom area in it. And then you'd go in there and you'd eat your breakfast. And after breakfast you'd drink coffee and smoke your cigarettes and start bitching about the company. And he'd listen. He did a lot a changes more or less for the contractors. And then he started getting bigger and bigger, and I think that's the biggest downfall of these guys. They get too big too fast. And, you know, they can't do nothing. I mean their hands get tied. They got to have too many people to run his business all the time.

Dan valued the personal contact with the boss and the courtesy of being taken to breakfast on a weekend when he and the other "contractors" were laid over waiting for Monday freight. But Dan left that company shortly after it merged with another carrier. It got "too big too fast," lost the personal touch, and became more regimented. Steve tells a similar story:

The man that started the company was named Bill. His brother was a bookkeeper, I guess it was for Meatpacking Company. The guy was a lush, but they tell me he was so good at getting their money back, or saving them money taxwise, that they let him stay drunk all year just for the time when they could take him back. Well, I guess it was through that connection with his brother that Bill decided to go into business hauling for the meat companies, and he started his truck company. He went in partnership with a guy by the name of John, who worked for a fuel oil company. I think he was driving a fuel oil truck. The company became very successful, and I guess John and Bill both became reasonably wealthy men.

To give you an idea of how these people operated, I'll tell you a story that happened to a friend of mine's father. He had made a trip for one of the owner/operators. He didn't have a truck of his own, but the guy wanted to take a week off, so he hired this guy to make a trip for him. He comes back. He's standing there around the garage, the old Reston Avenue garage there in Chicago, and Bill comes by and he says, "Why aren't you unloading?" He says, "I don't own a truck." He says, "I just made a trip for such and such a guy." He said, "Well, we've got a truck down there at the Smith Tire Company. Why don't you go down and get it?" He didn't even know who he was talking to and sent him down there to get this truck, gave it to him. The guy paid for it, you know, eventually, but he sent a guy down to take out at that time I guess it was a nine-ten thousand dollar tractor. He said, "We've got a truck down there. Go get it." They bought tractors. They bought trailers for guys right and left. And a good part of the time the guy drove off with them. They would bend over backwards to help an owner/operator. That's the way Bill was. (That's pretty unusual, I guess.) Very unusual. Very unusual.

But there was a company that later went downhill as far as their treatment of owner/operators. (Oh, they did?) Oh yeah. (They changed?) Yeah. Towards the end when I was there—one of the reasons I left was because of the way they were doing things. (How did it change, Steve?) Old Bill got old. I think he also died. I think so. And John he just wanted to get out of the business. His wife had died. He had two teenage or maybe early twenties boys, and they had no interest in the business. All they were interested in was reading books about stock cars and speed and stuff like that. And he just wanted out. And so they turned it over to some more or less the Joe-college type—no offense intended—and the papers and the CPA types. And the entire attitude between management and the help changed.

Steve, like Dan, tells a story of a change in the personal feel of a carrier due to a change in ownership. Interestingly enough, the change that Steve describes is probably a shift in the direction of "good business practices"—more systematic management, less particularism, and so on. From Steve's point of view, though, the change involved the importation of aliens (Joe-college types) and a shift in the "entire attitude," changes that caused him to leave.

Similar changes in the personal tone of a carrier, like the one described in the following excerpt from Irv's interview, come about as a result of a single employee rather than a wholesale change in ownership.

> Leo was the president, but his father's the one started the business. And when he retired he gave part of it to Leo, part of it to his wife, and part of it to his wife for his younger son, which was Irving. Well, Leo was taught the business by his father. When he come into that business he put him out on the dock sweeping the dock. Then he had to start working his way up from there. Then he had to go out in the shop and learn what was going on out there. In other words, when he got to be president of that company he knew every aspect of it, including he drove a truck, delivered freight. He knew it all. Now he was a good man to work for, because he couldn't tell you to do anything he hadn't already done himself. Well that was a beautiful job. Then Irving came back from the war, Korean War. And he came back vice-president in charge of operations, and he didn't even know what a truck looked like. Well, things wasn't the same anymore.

Irv goes on to describe the specific situation that eventually led him to leave the carrier. As he described the problem elsewhere, Irv found himself in the presence of people where "he thinks his word is law and that's it, nobody can reason with him." Red is another example of an independent who changed carriers because of a particular employee:

> Well, after I'd been there about three years, Vance quit or something, I don't know. He decided he was going somewhere else to work, anyhow. And the guy they brought in in his place, it just was a totally different atmosphere, and I didn't care all that much for it. So I'd gotten to be friends with the terminal manager in Boston, or in a town right outside of Boston. This guy represented a refrigerated carrier out of Texas. They hauled a lot out of meat out of Texas up into New England and New York. They took all kind of stuff back to Texas. And once in a while they'd run you to the West Coast and all that. So I signed on with them and worked for them for about two and a half years, almost three years.

Vance, the terminal manager for a carrier in Baltimore, was described earlier in Red's interview as the key to making the carrier a good place to work. He was not rigid about procedure, he kept the drivers loaded and running, and he straightened out any problems with the settlement sheet. When Vance left Red left to work for another carrier where he already had a tie of personal friendship.

Sometimes independents, like Ike in the next excerpt, describe the general management tone of a carrier rather than specific individuals who are responsible for it:

> One day I decided I get legal and went over there with Marathon Freight Lines. Stayed with them seven years. I made the money. One day—so they told me that, "Well, we got to keep in touch with you if we want to know where you're at every twenty-four hours, seven days a week. We want you to call in here tell us what you're doing." And I told them no. "My daddy was dead and my momma lived in North Carolina. My wife lived in Baltimore, and I didn't report to them every twenty-four hours telling them what I was doing. Why should I report to you?" So I left them and I started back and got on my own hauling freight. And I been making it ever since.

In conversation, Ike said he made much of his money by running heavy, that is by exceeding the weight limit (eighty thousand pounds in most states). When payment is based on the total weight in the trailer, the strategy makes good economic sense. Ike did well, buying a house and purchasing a new tractor. But the owner of Marathon started to worry about one of his trucks being in frequent violation of the weight limit. For whatever reason, the company wanted more control over Ike's trips, and as he states above, its demands caused him to leave. Carl made a similar comment on this kind of "regimentation":

> When the war was over, I decided to come back to Baltimore. I quit driving the tank and went to work for BC lines. That was like probably '45, '46, around in there somewhere. [interruption] I worked for BC, I guess about year and a half, maybe two years. I just didn't like the regimentation in the company. You had to be here at a certain time and show up there at a certain time. And I just wasn't used to that. In the milk tanker we knew we had to be where we had to go eight o'clock Wednesday morning. And if you wanted to leave Sunday afternoon that was fine with them. ('Cause they didn't really care how you got there.) Oh, they didn't care. As long as you got the job done and they knew you wasn't out running around in the truck and drinking and stuff like that. They didn't care as long as you done alright.

Carl expresses the same annoyance as Ike over the control of aspects of scheduling that he sees as his prerogative. At the same time, Carl recognizes that the carrier does have a legitimate interest in an independent's not attending to business ("running around in the truck") and disregard for safety ("drinking and stuff like that").

Independents, like most people, evaluate the human qualities of the workplace. They value honesty, fairness, the attributes desirable in anyone—in carrier personnel ranging from dispatcher to company president. Dan's story illustrates the value of the carrier's willingness to hear opinions and act on them. Irv's story shows the importance of the supervisor understanding the work because of his own experience. The qualities of one's employer are important to any worker, but when those people control your freight, your rates, and your paperwork, their character is even more crucial to your well-being, especially in a world where institutions provide no protection.

After finishing the interview with Steve and Dan around midnight, Dave and I walked out of the office toward the parking lot. Steve stayed inside to finish the paperwork on Dave's load and close up shop. Just before he climbed into his Freightliner, Dave told me what an exceptionally good dispatcher Steve was. He explained that Steve spent many years as an independent and knew what it was like. A supervisor's knowledge of the working world, whether through experience or the willingness to listen and act on the results of what he hears, obviously counts for a great deal.

In a class by themselves are some of Ike's stories about personalism. For instance, he describes going to work as the first black driver ever employed by a carrier in Florida. Because of a continuing problem with a white driver who was jealous of Ike's promotion to "road boss," he decided to quit and go off on his own after seven years. The boss and his wife are described as being hurt and upset by his departure, in a way that suggests the "ungrateful child" aspect of traditional white patronization of blacks. With only one black independent in this study, it is obviously impossible to perceive patterns. But it is clear that social and cultural differences, on the increase in recent times, will add new twists to discussions of personalism in trucking.

The Ugly Side

So far the independents have described this personal touch as an advantage, something that makes the carrier a better place to work. But some stories in the interviews bring out the uglier side of personalism, situations where the personal touch becomes a heavy hand. This version comes up several times, in Irv's story about a new dispatcher, or Dan's about an alcoholic one, or his general comment that some dispatchers take advantage of new independents and give them low-paying loads. A detailed example appears in Jack's story:

And then the day they fired me, I turned around and I parked my truck, because they wouldn't do nothing but give me one-way trips. They wouldn't get me back, you know, and I said, "I'm not going to do it no more." So I parked my truck out front. And I started pulling for common carriers again, running the company equipment. And the dispatcher lives up here in Blair, so he could drive past the house to see if the truck was still there. And he wanted to know what I was doing, how I was making my money to keep living, you know. And they seen the truck wasn't moved, and that was tearing them up no end. They couldn't figure out what I was doing, you know. So then he called me, and he wants to dispatch me and I told him no. I said, "Not until I got a decent run." They would always give me garbage, wouldn't give me a decent load to pull, so I wouldn't pull them. So then one day he says, "You're working for somebody." I said, "I ain't working for nobody." I said, "If I'm working for somebody, prove it, bud." I said, "When you can prove I'm working for somebody," I said, "then you got me." I said, "But other than that, my truck sits right out front here." I said, "You can ask my neighbors. You ask anybody you want." He says, "Yeah, we know it's sitting there." I said, "Then what are you asking me stupid questions for?"

And then I went down to the terminal to talk to him. And then they called me a goddamn liar. He looked just like you. In fact, you look a lot like John, I swear you do. And John was in the office. We got a little dispatch window about that big, and a little hallway that you walked into. And they had that office all closed off. And he says, "You're a goddamn liar, Jack." He says, "You're working for some-body." And I looked at him, and I said, "What did you say?" He said, "I called you a goddamn liar." I said, "That's what I thought you said." And two drivers tried to pull me back out of that window. I got caught in the window, I'd got myself hung up in there. I tried to get through at him, the dispatcher. I tried to get a hold of him. And his boss was his uncle that ran the whole steel division in Pitts-burgh, see. And his brother—the brother to the head guy—is the head honcho down at the factory that gives all the freight out. (So you were dealing with the whole family there.) That's right. And you know I hurt the one, the rest of them going to jump on me, you know.

So I got home here, and his uncle called me up from Pittsburgh. He said to me, he said, "Jack, I understand you threatened my dis-patcher, my nephew down there, the terminal manager." I said, "Well, let me put it this way to you Ron"—his name was Ron Hall. I said, "Mr. Hall, let me tell you one thing right now." And I says, "I ain't for no ifs, ands, or buts, and I ain't bullshitting you one bit." I said, "If you so help me ever call me a goddamn liar like your nephew called me," I said, "I'd come right out there right now and jump in my car. I'd run right out there personally and punch you right in your goddamn big mouth, too." I said, "Don't call me no goddamn liar. Nobody's got the right to call me a liar unless he can back it up." And he said, "Good, you're fired." I said, "Good." I said, "Then we'll see about it when we go to the union. That's because I'm definitely filing a grievance against you." And I got all my papers in there yet, ain't I hon' [to wife]?

So then I got my job back over that. Yeah, I got my job back over that. I went and stood before the board, you know, the union board. Well, we went to Pittsburgh. I made a trip up by automobile. I stood before the what is it—six men. Three company officials from different companies that sit on the board, and three union officials. And then the company presents their case against me, and I, you know, tell them what I—so I got my job back because they couldn't prove I was wrong, see. But then they were really laying for me. They were laying for me good after that, you know.

Jack's story about harassment brings the circle back to the problem of permanent lease carrier control over the load. Personalism turns ugly when a carrier uses its power and control over the independent's livelihood to harass or punish him. It becomes more annoying if the independent thinks he has a "reasonable" case that the carrier refuses to consider, as Irv exemplifies here.

See, the best part of it is you don't have to take a lot of bullshit off of nobody. But sooner or later you go to a place, you stay there for a while, they treat you real nice, and all at once then they're going to start getting shitty. (Why does that usually happen, do you think?) Well, one of my problems is this. I don't let them shit on me. When we was over at AC Transport as an example. [aside on previous company employee omitted] After we'd been there for little bit longer, things kept going up and up and up. And that's when the surcharge started. Julie had left in the meantime. Guy was there.

So I got Guy one day. I says, "Hey Guy, you go in there and talk to Rick. You want me to go and talk to him?" [He said] "About what?" [I said] "About the surcharge on these moves we're making." "Oh, we don't have to pay that." I said, "You don't?" I said, "Is an ICC number on the side of your trucks?" "Yeah." I said, "O.K., that's all I wanted to know." So I was standing there talking to the guys. Few minutes later Guy came back out. He says, "Wait a minute fellows, wait a minute." I said, "For what?" He said, "I was just talking to Rick. He's going to pay the surcharge."

In other words, they were aware of the fact no matter where I went that I'm not stupid. And I don't let them shit on me or anybody else that's working there if I can help it. If I see somebody else is getting shit on, I'll tell them about it. I don't mean the company. I'll tell the driver that he's getting shit on, and I'll explain why, and let him go to bat for himself. And companies don't like this shit, if you know what I mean. So therefore as a rule I don't last too long around these places.

Recall that earlier Will described carrier problems but then said he did not take action against the carrier because he did not want to be a "crusader"; Irv's description of what he sees as the consequences of demanding his rights helps explain why.

In a world where the carrier controls one's relationship to the market and where regulatory agencies and unions are not reliable allies, personalism becomes more important than just a normal concern with the human qualities of the workplace. It is a prime source of information to predict how things are going to go and what will happen when problems arise. Will you be facing an impersonal system of procedures with no knowledge of the details of your working world programmed into it, or will you talk with a reasonable dispatcher or manager who knows life on the road? On the other hand, a good system of impersonal rules might be better than a guy who comes after you with all the authority and control the carrier has because he doesn't like your looks. Personalism can cut through the rules, but in any number of directions. Sometimes rules would be an improvement.

Why go through all these problems? Why not take on some job with decent pay and some security? Because of the lure of the open road, the quest for the cowboy-like freedom of the open range? Before reaching those conclusions we must better understand how trips work. And once again, patterns of dependency appear throughout the stories in the interviews.

Chapter 8

Getting Underway

Load and Unload

An independent's trip involves more than just rolling down the road. At the beginning, something has to be put on the trailer, and when it ends, something has to be taken off. Seldom is he compensated for the time involved in actual loading or unloading, or for "detention time," the period spent waiting around at the shipper's or customer's. Depending on the type of freight, an independent may also have to do the actual work of moving freight on or off the trailer. If the load is "palletized"—arranged on wooden pallets or "skids"—he is lucky, because a "towmotor" or forklift can do the work at both ends. If he is hauling steel beams on a flatbed, a ceiling crane will do the work, though the independent will chain down the load and cover it with a tarp. On the other hand, if the load is forty thousand pounds of pears, then by the traditions of the produce world the shipper will load them, but the independent will "fingerprint" off eight hundred boxes at the customer's. (The ICC survey found that independents unload about half of their loads.)

On my trips, loading and unloading were typically uncomplicated: the shippers and customers did their work as quickly and efficiently as possible so that we could get back on the road. A couple of times we had to wait for the workday to mesh with our schedule; we arrived too early in the morning, too late in the afternoon, in the middle of lunch, and so on. One shipper employed one of the surliest people I have ever encountered. But on the whole, people were businesslike and friendly.

There were exceptions. We had a small shipment of forty boxes of toys to unload at a retailer's warehouse in Texas. Ike pulled around to the unloading dock while I took the papers through the receiving door. The drivers' area was a long, narrow room with a wooden bench along the wall, a couple of plastic chairs, a drinking fountain, and a pay phone. One wall had a plastic partition from about waist-height to the ceiling. Behind the partition sat the receiving clerk, a young man in his early twenties, busily signing forms, talking on the telephone, and giving instructions to several young women, some walking in and out of the office, some working at one of the several additional desks. Three company drivers were already in the room.

I walked in, slid the papers through the slot in the plastic wall, and told him we had a load of toys from XYZ. "Do you have an appointment?" "Yes," I lied. Actually, we had had one, but because of delays in unloading in a city two hundred miles distant we were a day late. The clerk consulted his book and did not find us listed. He told me to sit down because it was going to be a while. I said something about how he was going to ruin my whole day because my partner and I had to get to the Valley. Unlike the three company drivers, Ike wouldn't get paid for waiting to unload. The clerk consulted his book again, looked up, and said "door number three."

Ike backed the truck in and we both returned to the drivers' area. The clerk told Ike that it would be some time before they could unload us. As I understood it, they had to have one person to unload the boxes onto pallets and another to check the load, and they were short on people and long on trucks. Ike told him we would be happy to offload the boxes onto pallets ourselves. No, an employee had to do it. Ike told me to "be cool and watch" while he figured out a plan to deal with the situation.

Ike joked a bit with a young woman who was running in and out of the office. As she was leaving for the warehouse area, he asked her to "come here a minute." We all walked through a door into the warehouse area and Ike told her that we had to go. If we could not get unloaded, he said, he would just have to pull the truck up a few yards, put the boxes on the pavement, and leave. Then he teased her some more and we went back to the drivers' room.

For about twenty minutes Ike and the older drivers sitting in the room told stories about different loads they had hauled. The two younger ones sat quietly and listened. The theme of the stories was loads that were mysterious—the shipper put them on and when you arrived you found out that you had to have an armed military escort before you opened the sealed doors, or you were checked for radioactivity by a white-suited guy with a geiger counter. "They never tell you what they're putting on your truck," complained one. The younger driver turned to me and told me that he had an appointment for the previous morning and he was still waiting. He said he called his dispatcher and the company was raising hell with the receiving clerk. Little wonder that the company was raising hell; they were paying their driver an hourly wage for sitting in the drivers' room.

The young woman with whom Ike had spoken opened the door and told us to come in. They were ready if we would put the boxes on the pallets for them. I pulled the boxes from the nose of the van to the door, and Ike stacked them up. In a few minutes we were unloaded; the tape had separated on one of the boxes, and she noted that for a possible claim later. (None was filed.) She took the papers inside for the young man's signature. Signed papers in hand, Ike pulled the truck forward; I closed the van, and off we went to the Valley.

As we drove off, Ike said that the receiving clerk was going to be "red tagged" by the carriers as a problem. He guessed that from the looks of things, he had too many jobs to do with not enough people. Carriers were going to continue their complaints as long as their drivers were held up like the three we had seen. As far as how Ike handled the problem, he just said "you got to know what you can do and what you can't do." He said that if an hour or so had gone by, he would indeed have dropped the boxes on the pavement and left. According to Ike, he would have been perfectly within his rights to do so. None of the company drivers showed the slightest annoyance at our moving in ahead of them. But then they were being paid for waiting, knew that we would need only a few minutes, and realized that as independents we were losing money waiting.

Loading and unloading delays do happen, and when they do they freeze the independent's revenue. He makes money only when he is loaded and moving. Several stories in the interviews described loading and unloading problems. Red talks about delays he experienced at steel mills in years past:

Back in those days [1964], steel haulers particularly were treated pretty shabbily, really. It was nothing uncommon to go to a steel mill to pick up a load, sit there for four, six, eight, ten hours. And of course, you're working on a percentage of the total revenue for the load, so you didn't get paid hourly wages for sitting around like that. It was strictly on your own time. And this carrier particularly, very cheap rates. And I guess that's how they got all their business. I know it is, as a matter of fact. So anyhow, for, oh, about two weeks they ran me back and forth to Pittsburgh. I'd take a load up one night, bring another load back the next night. Time you made two rounds like this, sit around the steel mill for half the afternoon and waiting for your load, time you put in about four days like this, why, you're pretty well whipped out. But I wasn't really making enough money, and then they started running me up into New Jersey and eastern Pennsylvania, most of the time deadheading back. So I was really in bad shape moneywise.

Red's story sums up the "detention time" problem. The independent is paid on a percentage of the revenue for the load; the detention time is his unreimbursed problem. (According to the ICC survey, only 4 percent of the respondents were compensated for detention.) For part of their interview Steve and Dave swapped stories about loading and unloading problems. They teach us that detention time is all the more annoying when it results from the incompetence of others:

> Dave: But anyhow, this guy's truck broke down. Supposed to have this load of peaches in Chicago eight o'clock on this morning that he called me and asked me would I take the load up there, 'cause I called him and asked him about a load. I said, "Sure, I'll take them." They said, "You got to have them there at eight o'clock tomorrow morning."
>
> Steve: Famous phrase in the trucking business. They got to be there.
>
> Dave: We went down, transferred the load, and I jump in the truck. It's about four o'clock in the evening. And you know, I got this little motor here. And I drove all fucking night and stopped up on the Indiana turnpike. I thought, "Well, I'm gonna run in here to the service plaza, you know, and get me something to eat real quick." So anyhow, I went in there at the service plaza to get something to eat. Come back outside. Somebody done tore the mirror, turn signal, and every fucking thing off the left hand side of the truck. Sideswiped me. And, of course, they was gone. So I didn't have no mirror over there or anything. You know it's pretty hard driving one them sons a bitches without a mirror, even if it's on the driver's side. I don't know what I'd done if it'd been on the right side.
>
> Steve: Just hang your head out the window.
>
> Dave: Yeah, I'm going to change lanes. Let's see. Yep. Nope. Nope. My God, I almost run over that up there. So anyhow, make it on in to the truck stop, get me a mirror, stick it on there, you know, and go busting ass over there. Pull up to the store, five minutes till eight. Go around inside and look up the guy I got to see. And he says "Well, . . .
>
> Steve: "Park it outside."
>
> Dave: "Take it up there the end of the building. You may as well lay down and go to sleep for a while. Ain't going to get you backed in here for a couple of hours." Three hours later he gets me backed in. So they get me backed in there, you know, and I have a hard ass guy who helps me take it off the truck. Little back after twelve and now I'm unloaded ready to go. First the guy that does the checking. And I wait, and I wait, and I come to find out he's one of them four guys standing down there leaning on that tower of crates chewing

Independents Declared

the shit. Well by the time I realize which one he was, it was lunchtime.

Steve: Now he can't.

Dave: Now he's got to go to lunch for an hour. So he comes back. And by the time he gets back it's one-thirty, quarter to two, somewhere along in there. Well, then he had to talk to his buddies down there at the end about the football game, you know, who's going to win the football game. Had to place the bets on the football game. Quarter till three he takes time out to sign my damn delivery receipt. I mean, all he had to—he stamped it and put his initials on it. That's all he did. He didn't even sign it. He just stamped it and put his initials on it.

Steve: Tell me about it.

Dave: Standing there making goddamn fourteen dollars an hour. Too busy talking to his buddies to sign my fucking bill.

Steve: Mike, this may sound like exaggeration, but that's a common occurrence in the trucking business. And no matter how hot tempered you may be—you want to punch the guy—you keep your mouth shut, because you need that signature.

Dave: And you say one word to him and man they just take . . .

Steve: They penalize you. Then they lose the bill or something, or we got to check something out before we sign. You know, you can get yourself for more hours involved. This has been going on for centuries.

Dave: You say something, the next thing you know, well, they're over there with thermometers or something, you know. And, "well now, this is five degrees hotter than it's supposed to be, or it's four degrees colder than it's supposed to be. Ah, we don't want it. Take the whole fucking load and get it out of here."

Dave's "hot load" turned into a day of waiting to be unloaded. Because he finished in the late afternoon, he could not begin to look for a new load until the next morning. Had the customer unloaded him early, as he had expected, he might have found a load and been able to get on the road by evening. The delay costs him money. Steve vouches for the story, either by anticipating Dave's lines or by explicitly agreeing. The next story describes the potential damage a customer can do by holding up the paperwork:

Steve: I ran a load of beef into Philadelphia one time, I was there like one-two o'clock in the morning. The place was not open. They wouldn't open till maybe five or six. Dark. God was that a dark, old gutted place. It was reasonably safe. I used to put the back end of the trailer up against the dock so nobody could open it. Well, they took the load off in reasonably good time. An hour and a half later I was sitting there waiting for the guy to sign the bill. Then the old man started to chew my ass out because the color of the fat was wrong. "What are you telling me for? I didn't buy that crap. I'm not the grader. What're you telling me about the fat's the wrong color?" [He said,] "It's not the right cattle, not the right size." [I said,] "Don't tell me." He says, "I may just put it back on here." [I said,] "Not on this truck you don't." The guy had my bill laying there on the desk. And I saw it. And he saw me see it. He picked it up and put it in his pocket. And that touched me off like a firecracker. I said—can I cuss on that thing? (You can cuss all you want.) I said, "You can stick that bill in your fucking ass. I don't need it." And there was a guy standing there with a homburg on and an overcoat with one of them velvet collars on it like. He says, "Hey, that's a customer." I didn't know. He was the meat broker. He represented the meat broker from over in Camden. He happened to be over there. "You don't talk to a customer that way." I says, "Goddamn." I said, "I've waited an hour and a half for that bill. The meat is off. I don't need that bill." And I walked off, and it took six months to get paid for that load.

    Dave: Yep. They got you over a barrel and they know it. (And it's typical, this kind of shit?)

    Steve: Typical, oh yes.

    Dave: It is a definite exception when it's any other way but that.

The story isn't typical. They say it is to highlight their dependency.

Steve and Dave tell other stories that show reasons for delays. For instance, one story is about requests to repalletize a load, again with no compensation for the time involved. ("Repalletize" means shifting the load from the pallets it came on to different-sized pallets used at the customer's.) There are also stories about poor dispatching as a cause of congestion at a customer's, or even as a cause of arrival at the wrong time or even the wrong day. There is also the possibility that another driver might sneak in ahead of you if you relax your attention while waiting in line.

The main theme, though, lies in the independent's dependency on shippers and customers for getting the freight on and off the truck. He can't start a trip if the shipper delays him, and he can't put on another load until the customer takes the freight. With the customer the dependence is heightened; the independent cannot get paid until the customer signs off on the paperwork.

Lumping

"Lumper" is an unattractive term for a person who helps unload the truck. "Lumping" has been a problem for independents for years, because many places required him to hire the lumper they provided, whether he wanted one or not. After the independent truckers' shutdown in 1973, their testimony in Congress and agency hearing rooms succeeded in getting an "antilumping" clause in the Motor Carrier Act of 1980. In the next story from Steve's and Dave's interview, they describe some changes that have come about as a result of the new law:

Steve: They make a big thing about the—you've heard the term lumpers, I'm sure. Well, this is like all of a sudden it's a revelation from God. There's guys out there who's scalping the truckers. That's been going on for years.

Dave: Yeah, you know the thing that pisses me off, though, is they're all out there collecting their unemployment, and then they're coming down there charging you forty-fifty bucks to unload your truck, making that on top of their unemployment and shit.

Steve: I've asked Internal Revenue guys why they don't check on that. Most of these guys aren't even reporting that as income, but they never follow up on it. What are they afraid of? There used to be a guy unloaded us up in Jersey. I was trying to think of the name of that company we used to deliver to up in New Jersey. They're out of business now. But the guy that used to unload us was named Mickey. That was the name he signed your receipt with. He told me one day, he said, "My name's not Mickey." I can't remember what his name was. He was a New York City fireman, and he used to come on over there, and he'd pick up twelve hundred bucks a week unloading trucks. And then he worked around that meat packing house for a while. Nice guy. He was the nicest lumper I ever ran into. The only one that ever bought my breakfast. The only one that ever gave me anything other than a hard time. (Has it made any difference since the Motor Carrier Act of 1980? They made a big deal out of lumpers.) About lumpers? They're still out there.

Dave: What did it do? The only thing it says is you can not go into a company—they cannot force you—if they require you to have two people on your truck unloading, they must provide one of them. I mean it says they can not force you to hire someone. That's all it says. I mean, you either got the choice of driving two days straight to get there, and then you got the choice of either you get in there and you unload it yourself, or else you hire somebody. And if they require two people to be on the truck to unload it, they furnish one of them. They can't charge you for that one person. [exchange deleted]

Steve: You know, I'm telling you, Mike. I've handled a lot of freight in my day, but really the way it should be—the best for all concerned from a safety standpoint and from just fairness—the way that freight really should be is that the guy drives and that's all he does. Especially with this meat business. When you get there they should take that load off. There's no reason to ask a man to drive five-six hundred miles overnight, and then when he gets there (he's got to unload the truck) to the time schedule you want. He's to unload his truck or hire somebody at a hell of a rate to do it. That's wrong.

Dave: As far as I'm concerned, all shippers should load the trucks and all consignees should take it off. It's their freight. If they want it let them get it. That's just like why can't you set it up to have a standard—ship it on pallets, take it off on pallets. I mean, you know, that would really take just a whole bunch of cooperation.

Steve's comment about lumpers —"what are they afraid of"—is particularly interesting since lumping is sometimes said to be linked with organized crime. (See Brill, 1978, for a discussion of the situation in New Jersey, the setting of Steve's story.)

I was mistaken for a lumper at a produce terminal in New York. Red, Dan, and I were in Dan's truck delivering a load of pears from Oregon. We were all tired, but especially Red and Dan who had been codriving continuously since Nevada. As we pulled into the produce terminal and slowed to pay the seven-dollar admission fee, a couple of young men ran alongside the truck waving at us. They were lumpers looking for fifty dollars or so to unload. With three men on the truck, of course, Red was not about to hire a lumper.

After we found the customer and backed into the dock, Red went inside with the papers, Dan took off to find a bathroom, and I walked up to join three men warming their hands around an open fire. One said to me, "you come in with the truck?" I told him yes, and he, figuring I must be a lumper from outside, tried to talk me into hiring him to help me for twenty dollars. I declined, though after we finished unloading I wished I had thought it over first.

Red had hurt his back in an escapade at a Pennsylvania scale (see chapter 9), so Dan and I unloaded the 950 fifty-pound boxes of pears onto pallets. Later, Red told us that the man who ran the place came out, watched Dan and me at work for a while, and (assuming we were lumpers) said, "Hey those guys are pretty good; how much you have to pay them?" Red reports that he said, "Well, the guy over there owns the tractor," at which point he looked surprised. Then Red said, "And the other guy has a Ph.D. in anthropology"; he only missed a couple of beats before he said, "Oh he's writing something about how you guys get screwed over, huh?" I still haven't figured out if that was a comment on my proximity to truth or on the strength of what he felt was an anthropological bias. I think the former, since we were three days late due to a breakdown and a claim was in the air. It eventually was filed, and Red was penalized one dollar a box; the original revenue, before the broker's 10 percent and the home carrier's 7 percent was $3.50 per box. The claim reduced the gross for the load from $3,325 to $2,375, Red's share (before deductions and chargebacks) from $2,760 to $1,971. Even ignoring the deadhead miles from Portland to Medford and New York to Baltimore, the cents per mile rate is not worth figuring.

Maneuvering

The main point of these loading/unloading stories is shipper and customer control over the independent's livelihood, but some other stories inspired by the loading/unloading topic are worth mentioning. Some focused on difficult spots to maneuver the truck into, difficult because they were built for the "old days" when trailers were twenty-eight feet instead of forty to forty-five feet long. Other spots are difficult because the physical layout leaves little room to maneuver and is in the midst of traffic. Here's an amusing story about a difficult spot that Steve told on himself:

> This packing house in Cleveland sat higher than the load. And between the street and the packing house was the railroad siding. They used to load rail cars in front of it. Well for years we hauled out of that packing house. And there was a pole right there by the road that you had to skin in real close to that pole in order to get into the door where you loaded. I had a trailer that leaned to the left a little bit. That son of a bitch always was sitting like that. And it was tipped into that pole. The only thing was the wheels set all the way on the back end and there was a little bit of slope in the dirt away from that pole. And just as the top of the trailer was getting ready to hit the pole, the wheel hit that dirt and it would tip it away, you know. And the son of a gun would slide right in there. You could skin right past that pole and if you'd hit it right you could shoot right up against the dock in one shot.
>
> But it was a pain in the ass, especially if it was some traffic when you were trying to watch the other mirror because they wouldn't give you the break, you know. They'd try to pass you on the right hand side—with the ice and snow out there—and your trailer would start to slide on the slope a little bit. We used to say, "Why in the Christ don't they move that pole or take it down? Why's it have to be right there?" So they moved the pole. Couldn't hit that fucking dock to save my life. After they took the pole down, couldn't do it. That must have been a guide post or something. Before you could skin past that pole and put that son of a bitch in one shot. They took the pole down—all the room in the world you couldn't get in there.

Most of the truck maneuvering that I saw took place in large enough areas. (Though after the day I spent working in Baltimore with a tractor-trailer, the old skiis-in-the-revolving-door problem looked simple by comparison.) But some were crowded, small spaces off narrow, busy streets that were truly difficult, at least as indicated by the number of moves the driver needed to back in. After a while he learns to ignore the honking four-wheelers; there is nothing to do except get the trailer against the door as quickly as possible.

Steve and Dave traded another series of stories that combine difficult places to back into with the characteristics of the drivers who try to handle them. They told stories about a 115-pound woman who backed in better than most men, about Texas team drivers who always had trouble, about a pair of brothers who after thirty-five years in the business still asked people to back in for them, and finally about how it doesn't matter anyway because you only do well when nobody's paying attention. The stories are enjoyable and educational to nontruckers in that they describe some of the characteristics of a space that make loading and unloading more or less difficult from a driver's point of view.

Loading or unloading, if my experiences on trips were at all typical, is usually straightforward, though if the driver (not to mention the researcher) has to do the work it is still exhausting to be stuck with the job before or after a long run. But he never knows for sure. He runs into problems, delays, and exasperating situations caused by the shipper or the customer. Delays mean sitting for hours, even a day or two, and sitting means losing money. If he annoys a customer, the customer can hold up the papers, and he may not see his money for some time. And if the customer files a claim and wins, even though the driver has made his best effort it results in a direct cut from his check. Once again, the stories emphasize the independent's dependency on others.

The Driver's Log

After the freight is in the trailer, the independent fires up his "diesel car" and aims it at his destination. (Actually, if he is close to home he will probably load in the afternoon, go home for the evening, and leave before dawn the next day.) When he actually begins his trip, there isn't much about him, his truck, and his freight that doesn't fall under somebody's rules. The next chapter explores how some of these rules change as he goes from state to state. But first one should understand some regulations that travel along with him, visibly present at all times in the form of a booklet awaiting his attention.

The *driver's log* is routinely joked or complained about in the interviews, in conversations, and in the pages of independent trucker magazines. The log is designed to be a daily record of compliance with the hours of service regulations, found in section 395 of the

Federal Motor Carrier Safety Regulations. The details of compliance are so intricate that they can only be sketched here.

First, the driver must carry logbook records in the truck that go back seven days; he must submit a record to the carrier within thirteen days of its date. In other words, the driver must always carry the record of the past seven days, but if the log goes back fourteen days he is in violation. The home terminal may keep the logbook records until the twentieth day of the next month; the carrier must keep them in its principal place of business for six months.

The regulations are designed to limit drivers to sixty hours of driving time in any seven-day period, or seventy hours in an eight-day period. For a given day, a driver is allowed no more than ten hours of driving time following a period of eight consecutive hours off duty. If a driver has a sleeper berth, he may break the eight hours into two periods, as long as they are each longer than two hours. Finally, if "on-duty" time is mixed in with the driving time, the combination of the two cannot exceed fifteen hours.

This "on-duty" category is complicated. According to the regulation 395.2a, "on-duty" time is considered to be all time from the time a driver begins to work or is required to be in readiness to work until the time he is relieved from work and responsibility for performing work.

Now, the interpretation of what counts as on-duty time leads into what is called a "gray area." (At a meeting I attended one independent asserted that "the whole trucking industry is a gray area.") The regulations classify time involved in loading/unloading or working on the truck as on-duty. Riding in the passenger's seat is on-duty. So is sitting around the terminal waiting for a load. What about dinner at a truck stop? Who knows?

For the most part, then, an independent on a trip is usually on-duty unless he is in the sleeper. He can drive for ten hours and do other things for five, before being required to hit the sleeper for eight. This perversely adds up to twenty-three hours. Then every seventh or eighth day he must do no driving at all. Additional rules in section 395 cover who must keep a log, emergency conditions that allow rule violations, and additional details not relevant to this discussion.

To get down to cases, the log has a twenty-four hour grid on each page with four rows indicating "off-duty, sleeper, driving, or on-duty but not driving." The driver draws lines to indicate how he spent the day. Each time he moves from one row to another he has done a "change of duty," and must note the place where it occurred. The logbook must be current to the last change of duty, and it must also show the total miles run in the twenty-four-hour period to allow checking of his overall average speed.

Logs can be examined by several different state and federal authorities and in many jurisdictions by any local police officer. I have no idea what the range of penalties for logbook violations actually is, nor do I know how often logbooks are examined. In his interview, Jack told a story about getting caught:

(What does a fine run? What's an example?) Oh, it varies. I got nailed up in Michigan. I'd filled my log all the way out to the night before when I finished work. And I pulled out the next morning from the manufacturer. We slept there at the manufacturer that night. We pulled out the next morning, and an hour after I was driving they caught us for speeding up there in Michigan. And I had it all made out and everything, but I just hadn't struck my first line. So they fined me when I was stopped on the following day. I was illegal, so it cost me I think something like $28.45 or something, twenty-nine dollars. But hey, they can go up to a couple hundred dollars they can nail you for, depending on how they feel. And I had to pay the trooper right then and there. (You did?) Right then and there on the highway I had to pay him, out of my pocket into his pocket. Um hm.

Since the regulations require that the log show everything up to the last change of duty, Jack was in violation for not drawing his first line of the day across the logbook page. His story indicates his suspicion that the fine did not go much further than the side of the road, but there are, of course, other plausible explanations for the trooper's actions.

When independents talk about the log, one problem they often mention is that the delivery of loads requires violations. As Carl put it:

The worst part is—now I don't mind if an outfit's 100 percent legal, see. But don't come up with all this bullcrap, "Now this has got to be that way. This has got to be that way. And this has got to be that way. And that's got to be that way. And you can't do this and you can't do that." And then turn around and load you out of Chicago four o'clock in the afternoon, and say you got to be in New York six o'clock tomorrow morning. You know, now you got to break every rule and regulation to get there. But you can't turn in sixteen hours of driving on your log. You got to phony your log up, because they want you to be legal, but they done told you to break the rules, you know. Well, that just got me. Now if there was a carrier that was phony all the way, fine. Or if there was a carrier said you drive your ten hours and you to to bed, beautiful. But I ain't never found one like that.

Carl qualified his blanket statement in the next segment; once a carrier he trip-leased with required him to call in to insure that he was running a legal log, but he said that was the only time such a thing had happened. He elaborated on carrier pressures to run beyond hours of service:

> Three-quarters of the companies, you know, they all want to be legal, naturally, but you can't run an operation like that and run a legal log. Same way with Cleveland to Boston. You can't run Cleveland to Boston overnight legal. It's a thirteen-hour drive, hard driving, but I mean you can drive ten hours, eight hours off, and then another ten hours. Actually it's a twenty-four-hour legal run, but they want you to make it overnight. You'd be surprised what some of these companies—well, lot of times out of California they wanted fourth morning delivery. (To the East Coast?) Yeah, damn right. And if you didn't get there they'd start taking it off your revenue, miss the market, you know, and blah blah blah. And fourth morning delivery—'course you could probably do it now, you know, 'cause they got more powerful trucks and the roads are better. But in them days you know between fifty and sixty-five—Christ, fourth morning delivery, it was something else. 'Course I've done it a lot of times. Stay awake forever. (You'd have to.) Well, tough guy, you know.

In an industry where competition is in part in terms of service, carriers are frequently under pressure to get the freight delivered fast. If that pressure is handed on to the independent, as Carl describes it here, then he is caught between a rock—the hours of service regulations—and a hard place—the carrier.

Ike made another kind of comment about the logbook, one that the independent often expresses; if he follows the regulations he cannot cover enough miles to earn a living.

> (So you're saying you couldn't make a living if you were running a legal logbook, right?) No. Even if you working for a company you can't make a living running a legal logbook because you got to lie. With an owner and operator, that's what he got to do is lie. He can not make a living running a legal logbook. That's for a company with unions. That's when the logbook and all that mess started—after the companies had went into union and all of that—was to make sure that the drivers just only drive ten, take eight hours off, and only can travel so far. Then as of back in the '70s, they came out with the fifty-five-mile speed. You can't log over fifty miles an hour. You just can't make it. You can't make no living running a legal logbook. You can't make no living just running four-five hundred miles, sit down and sleep and all like that. When you load a load of freight them people looking for you to get it off. The quicker you get it off the quicker they get their money and the quicker you'll get your money.

When the log is checked, an officer can also check the total miles run. As a DOT official said in an independent trucker course, the policy is that anything over a fifty mile per hour average is considered excessive. With the ten-hour-a-day limit and the speed limit the driver could not cover more than five hundred miles a day. But as Phil points out, five hundred miles a day just is not enough. When the truck is loaded, the weather is good, the truck's running smoothly, and the roads are clear, the driver covers as much distance as he can. The hand of fate will slow him down soon enough, with a little help from shippers, customers, carriers, weather, traffic, and the fallible truck.

When Will talked about the logbook, he discussed how easy it is to get around the regulations.

> It's the same way with owner/operators. You're getting paid a low mileage rate, so guys are burning themselves out working trying to make money, because you got a low rate. And it's no problem to falsify a log, you know. It's a farce to start with. (One of the first things I learned is that—you know, owner/operator after owner/operator says you can't run a legal log and make a living.) No, there's no way. You can't make any money running a legal log.

Faking the log is a topic that everyone openly talks about (and writes about in independent trade magazines). One method commonly described is just to keep two logs, one constructed to be legal and the other reflecting actual work accomplished. But I learned an even simpler system. Its basis is simply that, over the long run, the independent will look legal anyway. Over a week he may have a few days of driving that violate the hours of service regulations. A couple of other days will be tied up in finding a load, getting loaded, getting unloaded, doing some work on the truck, getting caught in traffic or adverse weather, and so on. Another day he might be at home. Then even if he is pushing it, he will still stop for fuel and food and climb into the sleeper for a nap. If he takes the week as a whole, he can usually account for total miles run within the hours of service allowance. If he lets the log stay "a few days behind," things will even out. If the situation where the log is demanded allows him a few minutes in the cab to produce it, it doesn't take long to draw the lines across the page to bring it up to date. He just pretends all those delays took only a short period of time. This is not legal, since a lot of the time he does not show is considered "driving" or "on-duty, not driving," but he cannot afford to take a long rest when he is between points with a loaded trailer. He knows he will need time at the other end to find a load, and who knows what delays await him courtesy of Mother Nature, herds of four-wheelers, and his aging truck.

If so many independents are annoyed with the logbook, does it follow that they do not care about safety? Among those I traveled and spoke with, the answer is that the question is ridiculous. All considered adequate rest—and the problem of dealing with drowsiness while driving—to be a problem, and Carl and Steve explicitly discussed it.

In the course of my research, I encountered a bewildering variety of techniques for staying awake. The most popular is stopping for coffee. Some snack on sweets during a trip. One driver I met explained that by drinking three cokes before leaving the truck stop he was more effectively stimulated than by "pills." Another driver used legal over-the-counter stimulants. Yet another driver said he took one of his wife's "diet pills" when he first became tired, but then the next time he pulled over and slept. Most of the independents I talked with said they had tried pills, but used them seldom or never because of the side-effects. I did not set out to examine use of pills among truckers, but what I learned suggests that when such a study is done it will be complicated and will reveal that the stereotype of the pill-popping trucker, which is held by many truckers as well as the public, is overdone.

On the trips I took, when fatigue began to affect their driving, the independents pulled over and slept. They are as interested as anyone in avoiding accidents caused by fatigue. In general, the "folk safety system" must be reasonably effective, since as reported in a recent issue of *Heavy Duty Trucking*, driver fatigue "was a contributing factor in only 1.7% of accidents involving truck drivers reported to DOT in 1979."

The folk system, as I observed it, involves performance indicators of driver fatigue. A driver does not go from alert to exhausted in an instant. Subtle signs of fatigue first appear, such as variations in motor rpm's, indicating a decline in attention to pressure on the foot pedal; or slight drifting of the vehicle within its lane, signaling lapses in monitoring the tractor; or the body movements that accompany the two indicators mentioned above, such as rubbing the head and face with the hand. When these signals appear, it is time to rest; in my experience on trips drivers do so, with a couple of exceptions.

From the independent's point of view, the folk safety system has obvious advantages over the official hours of service regulations. The folk system implements a concern with safety while avoiding the contradictions brought into the cab with the logbook. It also allows for individual differences in the need for sleep and in preferred driving styles. Where a driver violates the folk system and pushes beyond the limits of safety, it is doubtful that the logbook adds any control.

No matter what the independent thinks, though, he has to take the log seriously, even though the time framework of the log does not fit the way trips actually unfold. But the regulators have the authority to require him to draw those lines, whether it makes sense or not. Like the stories about loading and unloading—stories that emphasized his dependency on shippers and customers—the description of the logbook brings out new dependencies with regulators, people who control permission to move the truck at all. And once the domain shifts from the federally required logbook to the question of what the individual states require, the madness increases to the level of the earlier discussion of rates. The American states, it turns out, are not always so united.

Chapter 9

State
by State

Truck Size

As an independent travels from state to state, there is little about him, his truck, or the freight he carries that is not touched by regulations. A variety of officials—federal, state, county, and municipal—can check for compliance as he travels the highways. The Department of Transportation regulates hours of service, truck standards, insurance, driver health and competence requirements, and so on. The Interstate Commerce Commission regulates the freight he can haul and where he can haul it, as well as the requirements for his lease, the sorts of papers he must have on the truck, and more.

In addition to the federal rules, an independent finds others that can change with each state line he crosses. Each state, at the time of this research, regulated the dimensions of his truck: weight, length, height—and each has its own rules concerning vehicle registration, state (as opposed to federal) authority, fuel taxes, and in some cases the "third structure" taxes, which require payment proportional to the number of miles run in a state, the amount of weight carried, or the number of axles on the tractor-trailer. State, county, and local traffic and safety laws differ too.

State regulation changes continuously. The Surface Transportation Assistance Act of 1983 requires states to follow federal standards in height, length, and weight requirements. Discussions of standardization of safety regulations are in the congressional air. It is not clear how this will work out, particularly since the issues verge on the fundamental constitutional question of the relationship between federal and state authority. In this chapter, "state-by-state" is discussed as it was in 1981–82. A 1985 update appears in appendix II.

In order to understand the gross weight limit problems, recall that independents haul low-rated freight that is usually high-density. In other words, the freight has a comparatively heavy weight per unit volume—steel, heavy equipment, and refrigerated meat, for examples. For this reason, a loaded trailer easily reaches the maximum federal limit of eighty thousand pounds. The problem is—or was at the time I did the interviews—that not all states would allow eighty thousand pounds of weight and sixty feet of overall length. Some interview segments dealt directly with this inconsistency, like this discussion between Steve and Dave.

> Dave: That's just like the states, you know. One state says you can be sixty feet long and you can weigh eighty thousand pounds. The next says you can be sixty-five feet long and you can weigh eighty thousand pounds. The next state says you can be fifty feet long and you can weigh 73,280. The next state says you can weigh seventy-three thousand and you can be sixty feet long.
>
> Steve: You know what Louisiana used to say? The steering axle is not a weight-carrying axle, and it's not used in figuring gross weight. They wouldn't weigh your steering axle when you come up figuring your gross weight, but gross is heavy weight. I mean that's where the trucker got a break, really. I doubt if it's that way anymore, but back in the '50s that was Louisiana's laws. Steering axle is not a weight-carrying axle, although you could move the fifth wheel and put a lot of weight up there.
>
> Dave: Well that's just like—now, you know, there are some states now that whenever they weigh your truck they weigh the tractor and they weigh the trailer. They take all three axles together. They don't weigh the drivers and the steerers and the trailer. They weigh the tractor and they weigh the trailer. They don't split the steering and the drivers. And so you've got, like say, forty-six thousand for the tractor, you know, the drivers and the steerers, right? They don't care where it's at. They don't care if you got fifty-nine thousand pounds on the steer axle and two ounces on the drivers or vice versa, you know. Well, they don't care if you got forty-six thousand-or forty-five thousand five hundred on the steerer axle and five hundred on the drives or the other way around.
>
> Steve: Who's doing that?
>
> Dave: Oregon's one for sure. Forty-six thousand.
>
> Steve: What do they do about tandem weight out there? Don't they go by tandem weight?
>
> Dave: Tandem weight thirty-four, but they weigh the whole truck at once. Let's see, where else is it? Iowa's going that way too, but Iowa's been doing some strange shit here recently. I don't know what they're doing, man. They have you split your drivers.

Steve: Oh, there's a lot of them splitting the axles.

Dave: They have you split your trailer axles. They'll have you weigh this and that. I came across out there one night, and they took about five different weights on the truck, you know. Weighed it this way and weighed it that way. And we were all legal, I mean all the way around, but they were just doing it for a survey-type thing.

To appreciate Dave's and Steve's discussion of weighing, recall that the typical tractor-trailer has a steering axle, tandem (two) drive axles, and tandem trailer axles. The allowable gross weight limits vary in different states, as do procedures for weighing the axles, which are critical in evaluating impact on highways. By Dave's and Steve's account, not only do states differ in weighing overall but in checking axle weights as well.

Recent history shows the reasons for the independents' annoyance. As of January 1981, the independent could run eighty thousand gross pounds anywhere, except for Indiana, Illinois, Missouri, Arkansas, Tennessee, and Mississippi. Unfortunately, that knocked out the middle of the country. Any shipment going across that block of states—the "iron curtain," as it was called—was legal at the shipper's and the customer's but illegal underway. To load legally for those states, the independent had to give up seven thousand pounds of revenue, and naturally the temptation is to load heavy and try to sneak by. (The frequently encountered 73,280 weight, by the way, was set as a condition of funding for interstate construction in the 1950s.)

States also differ in *how* they weigh, and some have different limits on different kinds of roads—turnpikes, interstates, primary, and secondary. Different styles of weighing come about because of all the possible axle combinations. The general federal guidelines are twelve thousand on the steering axle and thirty-four thousand on tandems, so a five-axle rig can be eighty thousand pounds. (Dave also mentions a "fifth wheel"—pronounced with the accent on "fifth"—but more on that shortly.) Some states weigh the overall gross, some, the axles and the gross, some split the tandems, and some use a "bridge formula" (not mentioned in the passage) that calculates different wheelbases between different axles to get the acceptable weight.

Weight is not the independent's only problem. State length requirements also vary. To illustrate the independent's quandary, he has a forty-five-foot trailer with a "cabover" tractor, the kind with the flat front. Cabovers, in fact, were designed to allow for more trailer with less overall length. "Conventionals" or "longnoses" with the engine out front under the hood increase the length. They also ride more comfortably because of the added wheelbase and have roomier cabs because there is no engine "doghouse" sticking up between the driver and passenger seats. (The 1983 legislation now allows forty-eight-foot trailers but does not limit overall length. Independents can buy conventionals without worrying about length limits. Industry publications are predicting that their use will increase.)

A forty-five-foot trailer with a cabover tractor brings overall length to about sixty feet. As of January 1981, the truck would be legal until it entered Missouri, Tennessee, Florida, West Virginia, Maryland, New Jersey, or Rhode Island. When it crossed those state lines it was five feet over length. Steve describes what can happen.

You know what the length is in New Jersey? You know what the fine is? One hundred sixty dollars, and they can get you for an inch if they want. That's 160 dollars. It was 200. Pennsylvania used to have a fifteen-dollar overlength fine. Maryland's thirty. A friend of mine—you would have loved him. Name's Frank. This guy was a character. He's another one of those guys that nobody in this world could be mad at. He bought a conventional tractor, had forty-foot trailer. Was running out of here with bananas. Run out of Cleveland here. He's breezing out here one day, going out towards Frederick, and they throw the tape on him. He's fifty-five, nine, or fifty-six feet, something like that. They give him a ticket. Back then I think Maryland was only fifteen dollars or something like that. It was a bit cheaper than the thirty dollars it is now. So he shortened up, and he left it shortened up even after he went into Pennsylvania. He had a lot of time so he figures he's going to run the mountains. Instead of going up the turnpike he went up through Route 2 or something. Got on 22 and was heading up 22 up toward Cleveland. He lived outside of Cleveland. He gets up there around Evansburg or something, and he sees this cop coming. Cop comes flying down there, jumps out with the tape. He said, "You're too late. They already got me down in Maryland, so I'm legal now." And then somehow or other he mentioned the fifteen dollars. "It ain't fifteen dollars anymore. It's a hundred and twenty," or hundred and fifty I understand. I said, "Holy"—Pennsylvania used to have a law that you couldn't pull a trailer over thirty-five foot in length.

(How in the hell did this mess ever come to be?) That's why I held the wallet up a while ago. It has to be for revenue, Mike. It's the only thing I can see. Do you know it's against the law in Ohio—it's a PUC [Public Utilities Commission] offense to drive with a dirty windshield. If they want they can ticket you for a dirty windshield. It was right in the book. I didn't believe that until I read it.

Steve's story deals with the length laws and the general increase in fines and taxes that are part of the new brand of state-by-state differences that is replacing the old one of length and weight. He closes with the theory that the density and inconsistency in the rules produce revenue for different jurisdictions, giving the Ohio PUC (Public Utilities Commission) example as a case in point. The historical themes of increased regulation and enforcement continue by his account.

Steve also talks about "shortening up," a procedure involving the fifth wheel. The fifth wheel is a round metal plate with a slot facing aft that sits at the rear of the tractor chassis. Near the nose of the trailer is a kingpin that slides into the slot and locks into the fifth wheel so that the tractor can pull it. To pick up a trailer, the driver centers the tractor and backs it underneath until the kingpin locks into the fifth wheel. He throws a safety switch on the cab control panel, then cranks up the "landing gear," the metal legs that support the trailer when it stands free, and goes on his way. Well, first he should check to make sure the connection is secure; there are stories about drivers who didn't. They pull away and drop the trailer on its nose, which is always embarrassing and usually expensive.

Details of a trip experience help to explain the fifth wheel. After loading the van with pears in Oregon, Red and I went to a scale at a truck stop to check the weight. Although the gross was just at eighty thousand pounds, the weight on the drive axles was a bit heavy and we had to adjust the weights. Red's tractor (like most) has a "sliding fifth wheel" mounted on tracks that allow it to be moved closer or farther away from the cab. He also has "sliding tandems" on the trailer, axles that can move forward or backward along perforated girders, held in place by retractable metal pegs. The trick is to use the brakes and engine to change the position of the fifth wheel and the tandems to redistribute the weight. Since the drive axles were heavy, we slid the fifth wheel forward to get more weight on the steering axle and the tandem axle forward to take on more of the trailer weight. Unfortunately, sliding the fifth wheel forward gives a rough ride. But after Red made the changes he drove across the scales again and presto, we were legal on all axle weights. The fifth wheel and sliding tandems are vehicle characteristics, like the cabover tractor, that are a direct response to regulations.

Inconsistent Details

The state-by-state weight/length/height inconsistencies will soon be history, although new ones described in the update (appendix II) are already replacing them. But there are other inconsistencies as well. Some involve local traffic regulations as in this account from Steve and Dave:

Steve: Like he was talking about, you know, this state allows so much weight and so much length. Have you ever noticed a truck traveling with their four-way flashers on going up a hill? In Pennsylvania when your speed drops below forty miles an hour, you are required to do that. Otherwise, it's about a thirty-five-dollar fine.

Dave: Fifty.

Steve: Is it fifty now?

Dave: Inflation, you know.

Steve: In Maryland it's against the law if you do do it. Then you can get a ticket for it.

Dave: Fifty.

Steve: Now, one of them's got to be wrong. Now here's two contiguous states. I mean you go from one right into the other. This one you got to. This one you can't. Up until a few years ago you were not—even though the new cars came out with flashers on them. That was illegal. The only vehicles that were allowed to have flashers in Maryland—well that's probably about ten years ago—were emergency vehicles and police vehicles. Trucks were required to have the four-way flashers by the Interstate Commerce Commission but Maryland did not allow four-way flashers on a truck by law. I never heard of it being enforced. And they were not allowed to be used on a car, even if you were broke down on the shoulder. You were not supposed to put four-way flashers on.

A trivial inconsistency? Spread it across the range of detailed traffic regulations in any jurisdiction and multiply it by forty-eight (and numbers of counties and towns) to get the general idea.

Paperwork

In chapter 4 Jack described many independents' annoyance that the permanent lease carrier takes 25 percent or 28 percent of their revenue. But one of the valuable services that the carrier does provide for that percentage is expertise and leverage in dealing with state documents, although in chapter 6 this same service provided opportunities for "carrier tricks" as well. Red describes the situation:

You asked about the permits, state permits, and so on. Well, you always buy your base [home state] license plate. The first company I worked for, the only permit we needed was, at that time, I believe you needed a West Virginia and a Virginia. All the rest of the states that we ran in—Pennsylvania, Maryland, Delaware, New Jersey—had reciprocity. They didn't require any cross registration. They didn't even require fuel tax stickers and stuff like that. They were reciprocal on fuel tax. So then when I went to work for A and C, we had quite a few other states to run in. And A and C charged us for the permits every year, until we got the union in. And then under the terms of the union contract—and that was standard in union carriers, that the company furnished all of those things. In all cases the carrier reports the mileage and taxes to the various states, which is part of what you're paying—you know, what they're taking their percentage out of the pie for. They don't all do it accurately. And I can tell you a little story on that later on and what it can lead to. But even with A and C, we were working strictly the northeastern part of the country and eastern Canada. And we had a lot of states with reciprocity with one another. So we had not that many permits to buy. And they were like a dollar or two dollars apiece and that sort of thing.

Then when I went with Southwestern, that was my first experience of course with a basically forty-eight-state operation. And, well, you had license plates and stickers plastered all over your truck. And by actual count, if I remember the figures right, when I was fully permitted for Southwestern—and that did not include an Oregon PUC [Public Utilities Commission] plate. So that would have been another one. But even without Oregon I had, as I recall, thirteen state license plates and twenty-three stickers on the truck, plus a book that looked like the family photograph album full of papers. And it was—well, as you found out yesterday, you know, dealing with that toadfish over there at the scale house, most states that you're running through you have to deal with three different divisions, three different departments within the state. So that's where you get into all that paperwork. So anyhow, Southwestern charged us back for everything.

Then we also had to turn in an original fuel ticket for each and every state that we ran in. And they had a guy sitting down there that did nothing all day long except count up how much fuel each one of the trucks bought in each one of the states, and the mileage that each one of them ran in each one of the states, and figure out whether according to an arbitrary miles-per-gallon figure you had bought enough of fuel. The idea being if you didn't buy enough of fuel, the company had to make up the difference when they reported to the state. So if you didn't buy enough of fuel, then that was a chargeback to you on your settlement. And this my first experience though with what happens when you buy too much fuel—more fuel than what you need to run the state. Somehow or another we never saw a refund.

The details in Red's description recall carrier tricks and problems in getting one's own authority. The independent cannot just drive through a state, even if he has federal authority. He deals with two or three separate offices to register his truck, get a fuel permit, and obtain authority. Many states also have the "third structure" taxes mentioned earlier—taxes based on miles run and weight carried, for example—that add additional fees and forms. Recently, these third structure taxes have increased in number, sometimes with the benefit of railroad-funded local political action groups. (See the May

1983 *Heavy Duty Trucking* special issue, "Railroad War on Trucks," for details.)

In their report on state regulation, the Department of Transportation (1981) dramatized the problem with two examples.

> In order to get authority to transport *exempt* commodities in 34 states, a trucker must complete *198 distinct* forms just to begin operation. This does not take into account any third-structure taxes, insurance certification or continuous filings for fuel tax reporting.
>
> A household goods carrier noted that to legalize *one* typical tractor and trailer for operation in 48 states for one year requires filing all applications and permits listed in Table I and writing 76 checks. *In addition*, 290 fuel tax, third-structure tax and miscellaneous mileage based reports must be completed for 42 states involving 32 different formulas and 48 different forms. If the tractor were driven 100,000 miles during the year the company would process approximately 300 log, mileage and fuel records and 285 fuel receipts. The fuel accounting requires a detailed audit as there are 34 sets of requirements in the 38 states with fuel tax reporting laws.
>
> (The first paragraph is from the testimony of Joy Fitzgerald; the second Kevin Lewis. Table I is a list of decals and forms.)

Dealing with this mound of paper is one of the services that a carrier provides. Usually the independent pays the fees, but the carrier will provide the proper forms and see that they are filed. Understanding the immensity of paperwork required illuminates Dan's annoyance, described in chapter 4, when he learned what his wife had to do to replace this carrier service. Under the reforms of the Motor Carrier Act of 1980 ICC authority is easier to obtain than ever before. But when the independent contacts the states through which he will regularly run (even assuming the most helpful of agency employees) he is in for a jolt. And the DOT report shows that even an exempt hauler, who does not need ICC authority, is still buried under state-by-state paper.

Dan's wife, who was in the middle of the process at the time, taught me about state applications. She had the ICC authority, and now she wanted permission to run in the eleven western states. She told me about the expensive bond that many states require before issuing a fuel permit, about the hours she spent on the phone just trying to get the right number of the right person, about the detail required in each state's reciprocal registration package, about paying for a service so that she and Dan would have a local address in each state, and on and on and on. She gave me the reciprocity forms for a couple of western states; it took me an hour to read them through; they were filled with shaking fingers warning that the form would be rejected if such and such was not filled out exactly right. Detailed information and estimates of mileage for the next year were required. Not surprising was Dan's opinion, expressed during our taped interview a couple of days later:

> I think I done pretty good. I mean, I can't really complain that the trucking world's really been that bad to me. But there is no money in this business anymore working for a company. You can make a little profit on your own, but there's just too much of this bullshit rigamarole—all of the different things that the states all want. You know, I mean you go out and apply for ICC authority and then you got to have authority for this state and authority for that state. You can't just, you know, run that ICC number anywhere. You got to get your authority to run through the other states. It's a bunch of bullshit as far as I'm concerned.

And in response to my usual end-of-interview question—was there anything that I should have asked about but didn't:

> Just wish the hell the ICC was a lot easier to get your authority shipped through a lot easier, and you wouldn't have to get all this go to each state and get everything according to each state. Stuff like that. You know, I mean every state's got a different deal and it's so goddamn hard to license and be able to, you know, to operate legally in every state without screwing up somewhere.

State by state. All the rules change even if the independent has federal authority. It is a source of conflict as old as the United States Constitution. Well-intentioned transportation experts often wonder why independent truckers have not rushed to the post office to send off their applications for authority. One answer that no one thought of (including Dan and his wife until they confronted it, or me until I learned about it), was that getting one's own *federal* authority is just the beginning. After that, the independent faces much more additional time, expense, and general craziness to get legal status in each of the states he wants to run through. It is not an impossible task, particularly if he wants to run through only a few states on a regular basis. But the inexperienced small businessperson without the personnel and leverage of the large carriers finds the process difficult and frustrating.

Harassment

The interviews have provided samples of a few of the things about an independent, his truck, and his freight that are subject to inspection. A police officer, weighmaster, or other official might look at the truck, the freight bills, the authority, the lease, the operator's license, physical exam certificate, vehicle registration, or driver's logbook. The kind of official who can demand these examinations varies from state to state and has changed over time, though most independents agree with Steve that "a lot of them aren't qualified; they don't even know what they're looking at." (Steve mentions these shifting enforcement roles and incompetences again, as do other independents.)

So many federal, state, and local authorities having the power to inspect so many things creates the potential for harassment. Dan describes how harassment is getting worse.

> Yeah, it's the harassment more or less, with, you know, your law enforcement and stuff like that there. I don't know. It's just, you know, some guys can be nice to you out here and some guys can't be. And a lot of them just think that we're easy money to get out of, so they harass us all the time. It's a lot more than it used to be when I first started. When I first started driving down here in the United States—you know, it's gone against us more than for us.

The earlier discussion of the history of trucking indicated that the regulatory web has thickened and enforcement of violations has intensified in general over the years. This policy trend is often talked about as a kind of harassment—a matter of policy to "get" the truckers. An increase in regulations and enforcement is, of course, different from harassment on a personal level. Ike ties the two together and describes the consequences for the independent's profits:

> (Was it real different then in terms of the regulations; the permits, and going from state to state, and all that kind of stuff?) Yeah, it was way, way different. (Can you talk about that a little bit?) Well, back in them days the states and all wasn't pushing you too much about permits. They didn't bother too much then about permits. Back in '40—about '46–'47—they started the logbook but they didn't push that issue too much until back in the early '50s. (Why did that start Ike, do you know?) Well, they claim that guys was having a lot of accidents and falling asleep. And they wasn't falling asleep. But with an owner and operator, you can't run a logbook and be legal, because your time pressures you. You got to load and unload. That's the name of the game in order to make money. So just a lot of difference now than what it was then, because now they hired a whole bunch of DOTs and all out checking your permit, wanting to look at your logbook. And they don't know what it's all about if you give it to them. Only thing they want is just the money. Any little thing they can get you with and fine you. So that's the reason why you have to get back in the woods and run at a certain time of the day, certain time of the night. You got to know what time they go to breakfast. What time they come to work. And know what time they go to dinner, and what time they go to supper, and then you do what you got to do.

Ike's comments on the increased enforcement of growing numbers of regulations echo the registration and enforcement stories from the old days recounted in chapter 3. Ike also talks about increased numbers of "DOTs" (state transportation officials, in this context) who are primarily out after your money, even though they do not know much about trucking. Only thing you can do, concludes Ike, is learn their schedules and avoid them.

I saw Ike's expertise in action several times on our trip. In one southern state (for which he was not permitted), we suddenly came up on a temporary sign on the side of the interstate that said, "all trucks stop ahead." Almost before I had finished reading it, Ike was off the interstate and onto the state highway. This ruse does not always work, because officers know the roads too, and may patrol them during a check. But in this case it worked very well. We wandered the back highways, passing through small towns in the company of a few other trucks, until we returned to the interstate near the state line. It was odd that Ike picked that moment to say, "not like *Smokey and the Bandit*, is it?" It seldom is, but at that moment I admit I felt like I was costarring in the sequel.

On my trips, I witnessed almost no harassment. Officials were professional and businesslike. When officials did give the independent a citation it was for a genuine violation of a regulation. From the independent's point of view, the regulation might have been nonsensical, or the violation, under the circumstances, might have been unavoidable, but he did not attribute bad intentions to the official.

Except for one weighmaster in the West. Red was legal in gross weight, so he did not expect any problems as we rolled onto the scale. To his surprise, the red light flashed, signaling him to park in the back and bring his papers into the office. Red had planned to stop there anyway. His permanent lease carrier was not registered in the state, so he needed to buy a trip permit for a single trip. As Red opened the door and preceded me into the small scalehouse, I heard his quiet "oh-oh." Behind the counter sat a person who just looked like trouble, and he was. We were there about an hour and a half, all told. He went through Red's permits, his bills, his license and physical card. He telephoned several offices to check for data on Red's permanent lease carrier. He interrupted several times to flag a truck on the scale—often on a whim—once because the name of the company was "Hot Damn" Trucking, for instance. He spent two lengthy phone calls chatting with a friend at the scalehouse on the other side of the interstate and arranging for their coffee break. Then he took his time filling out several forms to issue us a permit and fine us for not having one. With that, he looked up, smiled, and told us to go out and get our logbooks.

Red was a few days behind on the log, a common enough occurrence, as we learned in the last chapter. He sat in the cab, quickly filled in the missing days, and we walked back in. Then the weighmaster turned to me and asked for my log; Red explained that I wasn't a driver; then he asked for my written permission from the carrier to ride. Red's carrier knew about me, but written permission? Sure enough, the official pulled out a well-worn copy of the DOT regulations; with a rapid accuracy born of experience he turned to the page with rules that prohibit riders except in case of emergencies or with the written permission of the carrier. I got ready to improvise around whatever story Red decided to tell, but he just said straightforwardly who I was and what I was doing. I whipped out my faculty ID, tried to throw around some anthropological jargon, and attempted to look professorial, which was a good trick considering I was still pretty grubby from unloading in North Dakota. Anything was better than a bus back to Baltimore, and technically he could have required that.

Fortunately the weighmaster decided it was time to discuss some issues, among other things talking about how under Reagan the states would have even more control over regulation of trucking, which considering the circumstances, did not impress us. He also said he did not understand why drivers objected to the log since it protected them from overwork. Finally Red got his papers and paid a $150 fine and the $70 fee for the trip permit.

We walked out the door and began muttering profanities in stereo, the volume increasing with our distance from the house. Red's final comment was that the little houses next to scales were called "chicken coops" not only because of their structural resemblance to same, but also because of the characteristics of some of the occupants. We had been harassed. Later, we heard from a local driver in a truck stop that the weighmaster was a famous truck-hater. He told a memorable story about the time the weighmaster illegally reached through a window into a cab; the driver closed it on his arm and drove away.

For the most part, though, the officials I saw on the trips ran from straightforward and professional to "nice guys just doing their job." Some stories in the interviews even describe benevolent authorities:

Dave: You know what I did here back earlier this spring? I can't believe I did it yet. Claude and I were coming in off the Indiana turnpike. And we come out of the tollgate up there on the Ohio pike, and it's three o'clock in the morning. Ain't nobody out. Well, when they tuned our trucks up, they give me about an extra 200 rpm there, you know. And we've come out of the tollgate there. Ha. Mile marker number seven, man, I just got there back in a big hole and I'm getting it wound out really good. Dropped down around this little curve and around to the left under this underpass. Now about that time my fuzzbuster's coming off the dashboard. I mean, you know, there's a cop right there. He got me. Seventy-seven miles an hour. He got me locked in. So I knew he had me. He's over there trying to get through the guard rail and get turned around. I just went over there on the side and waiting for him. And Claude says, "I'll see you down at the next rest area."

So anyhow he pulls over there behind me. And I get out, take my permit case, you know. My log's about four or five days back. I walk back there and get in the car, and he says, "What's your hurry?" I said, "Aw, I had to show off my . . . big wagon here, dammit." He just kind of laughed a bit. And so he gets out, you know, and he just looks at my registration and driver's license, and then calls me in and checks me out on the driver's license and all that. And he talks to me all the while. He gets out his warning ticket book, and he says, "Well, I'm going to give you—no. Seventy-seven. I can't give you a warning ticket. Seventy-seven. Aw, I'm going to give you one anyway." He says, "I just want you to know"—he shook his book at me. He says, "Look. This book here"—you know, about as thick as a guest check book in a restaurant, and it's still over half of them in there. He says, "I've had this book for over two years, and there's still over half of them in there." And he gave me a warning ticket. Seventy-seven mile an hour. He says, "The next time you come through here"—I just couldn't believe I did that though.

Dave is not proud of going as fast as he did, and Steve's facial reaction supported Dave's verbal commentary—seventy-seven is too fast. (During most of my trips, a wide-open speed was about sixty-five. Seventy-seven is too dangerous and too hard on the equipment.) Dave explains that his engine had been tuned for two hundred more rpms and he was winding it up "back there in a big hole." A "hole" is a gearshift position, but a particular hole may be one of three different "gears" (on a thirteen-speed), depending on how the auxiliary and direct-overdrive are set. So Dave is "back there in a big hole," in other words, in the highest gear. The officer gave him an unbelievable break by writing a warning ticket, and he made a point of showing Dave his book of unused tickets. He is one cop who does not harass truckers. Steve told a couple of stories with similar themes, that some smokies range from "reasonable" to "nice guys." They are, after all, co-professionals of the road.

Federal Checks

Even though he is in state territory, an independent might run into an island of federal authority anywhere along the line. The Bureau of Motor Carrier Safety, formerly in the ICC but later moved to the Department of Transportation when it was founded in the 1960s, sets up stations occasionally to check safety regulations. States do this as well. Steve describes how they worked in the days when ICC did the checking:

> I crossed the bridge at Quincy, Illinois, over the Missouri, and there they were. This was like a back road. It was a U.S. highway, but it was not a heavily traveled U.S. highway. It was more like a minor U.S. highway. I never in my wildest moments would have ever thought that the Interstate Commerce Commission would be there. And I come across the bridge, and there they were. Nowhere to go but in. The guy that checked me happened to be an ex-greyhound-bus driver, and the funny part of it was I thought I knew him. Not that I knew any bus drivers, but facially he looked like somebody I knew. And he thought he knew me. But neither one of us could figure out where we knew the other from, and probably put us on a, you know, friendly basis like. And he pushed me through with just a minor check.
>
> (If they do a check—if they really do a number, what do they do?) If they do a number on you, they got the coveralls on. They'll go underneath and they'll check the travel in the slack adjusters. They'll check the brake linings. They'll check the springs. They'll check the frames for cracks. They'll check for leaks. They'll check for dangling wires, or air lines that are not properly fastened. Chafing on air hoses to the trailer, or to the diaphragms on the tractor or trailer.

Steve also described his experience of a less friendly check in which the state police officer working with the federal team ticketed him for smooth tires, tires he claims he drove on for another six months.

Some of the things that Steve describes are familiar even to the nontrucker (brakes, springs, cracks in the frames, wires); other items are related to the compressed air system—leaks, air lines, air hoses, and diaphragms—vital to the safe operation of the truck. Without air, the truck not only loses its brakes; many other components, such as the auxiliary transmission shift, the window on the rider's side, and probably the suspension on the driver's seat all run off compressed air. If a problem is dangerous enough, the inspector will "redline" the truck: not allow it to move under its own power until the problem is fixed.

While the time loss is annoying, most independents I have talked with see the value in such checks (though Steve told another story about the lengths he went to to avoid one). Like many other state-by-state issues, there is currently a move to standardize safety inspections, so that a sticker issued in any state will be recognized by the others. In conversation, Red described a state check in California that uncovered a mechanical problem that would probably have caused an accident. He was grateful it was found. As several independents said, in different ways, "There's a lot of junk running up and down the road." They do not sound any happier about that than would a safety inspector for the DOT.

Illegal Trips

If the independent is carrying hot freight, or slipping through a state without papers for it, or carrying some extra pounds to pick up extra money, the hassles on the trip automatically increase. When he is legal, checks of the vehicle or paperwork are just part of the game. When he is not legal, the game continues but at higher stakes. Some of the problems that can come up are illustrated by examples from the trip with Red. He had no intention of running illegally; the problems began when a broken crankshaft disabled his truck in Nevada, a story related in detail in the next chapter. Red found another independent, Dan, and offered him the revenue for the trip if he would hook his tractor to Red's trailer so we could get the load of Oregon pears delivered to New York City.

When we put Dan's tractor under the trailer, we were in trouble. The first problem was that the ground under the loaded trailer had thawed a bit and the landing gear sank down into it. Fortunately, Dan had "air bag" suspension and could raise and lower the back of the tractor using compressed air. We spent an hour using the air and some scrap wood to build up under the landing gear before we hooked on to the trailer.

The main problem was Dan's new conventional tractor, about seventy-five thousand dollars worth, with a "walk-in" sleeper—a good-sized box connected to the back of the tractor with double bed, hanging closet, and room to move around. All that luxurious room meant that we were well over sixty feet in overall length. We were also overweight, since Red's much smaller truck alone was right at eighty thousand pounds. With Dan's tractor, we later learned, we were at about eighty-two thousand pounds and sixty-two feet. Nice and illegal in most any state of the union. Neither Red nor Dan was happy about this, but Dan needed the work and Red had to get the load delivered. As independent after independent says, you do what you have to do.

We made it around the scales and ports of entry with no unpleasant surprises from roving inspectors until Iowa. At the Nebraska-Iowa line, Dan and I went into a truck stop for coffee—Red was sleeping until his turn at the wheel. Dan bought an atlas in the store and looked around; he went up to a driver, laid the map on the counter, and said, "Where are the scales in this state?" The driver immediately pointed out the ones we needed to worry about, and then Dan asked, "How do we get around them?" The driver pointed out the possibilities. Later Dan told me he asked this particular man because he was dressed in regular working clothes—"didn't have on a cowboy hat with feathers and all that shit"—and he was charging a purchase, which probably meant he was local.

We got past the first scale. Red and Dan were nervous because Iowa is apparently known as a strong state on enforcement, and because we had to run through during working hours on a weekday when more enforcement people are out. As we drove down a two-lane state highway through a small town, we all saw the powder blue car with "DOT" (state department of transportation) on the trunk. He took one look at us and pulled us over. He wrote us up for overlength and lack of permits, for a total of eighty-eight dollars. He was a straightforward officer, as Dan and Red later said. (I heard later, because I was told to get in the sleeper and stay out of sight. After the trouble with the western weighmaster, described earlier, I was going to do that anyway.) The officer was lenient because he did not take us to the scales to get weighed, which would have increased the amount of the fine.

Near the Iowa-Illinois line was another scale, and according to the talk on the CB it was closed. So we stayed on the interstate, but unfortunately found the scale open. (People say that some scalemasters turn the sign on and off just to confuse the CB messages.) We ran across the scales, and the scalemaster's voice came over the loudspeaker asking Red to come inside. Red took along the receipts for the fines already paid, hoping for the best. The officer was sympathetic and told us to get back on the road.

We got through Illinois and Indiana and were safe on the Ohio Turnpike, which charges tolls by weight. But then Red and Dan got into a debate. Red wanted to leave the turnpike at Youngstown and stay with Interstate 80 all the way to New York. Dan wanted to stay on the Ohio and Pennsylvania turnpikes where we would be protected from scales and overweight charges, and then drive the additional distance up to New York. Red won.

Our first problem was that as soon as we left the turnpike, we were supposed to have a square white Ohio Use Tax registration sticker in the lower right hand corner of the window. Needless to say, Dan, a western runner, did not have such a sticker. My job was to rig a square of paper about the right size and stick it on there, but I don't know that it would have fooled anybody.

We got into Pennsylvania and made it through most of the state. Red was fairly sure that we were past all the scales, although he said he had not run this way recently. Unfortunately, we rounded a curve in the mountains and there sat the new scale, the "Open" sign glowing neon-red. Needless to say, Red was told to park his truck in back and come in to the scalehouse. The fine was two hundred dollars. Then I learned that in Pennsylvania, like some other states, an overweight truck has to "get legal" before it moves. One way to do this is to call and hire one of the services that exist in such states to take off the overload and follow you to the state line, but that is expensive. While Dan and Red worked on shifting the fifth wheel and tandems and knocking off the accumulated ice to minimize the overload, they told me how to help solve the problem.

Every time I saw a reefer pull into the scale, I picked up the CB mike and said "How 'bout you eastbound reefer coming into the coop?" ("Coop" or "chicken coop" is the term for scalehouses.) If someone answered, I told him we had about fifty boxes of pears (twenty-five-hundred pounds) that we needed to get off; could they help us out? After about twenty minutes, a driver came around. He opened his trailer doors and backed up close to our open doors, and the three of us moved the boxes from one trailer to another. We arranged to meet somewhere down the road and he left. We went across the scale again and were still a little heavy, but the officer let us go. As we drove down the road, I occasionally called on the CB to find the other driver. He was parked behind a truck stop about fifteen miles away, and we just backed the trailers up to each other and reversed the process. Red asked him what he wanted, and he said he hated to do it but he'd take something. Red offered him a twenty, and he thanked us and left.

Fortunately, we crossed New Jersey late at night and arrived in the Bronx in the early morning hours. We would still be too long for New Jersey and Maryland as we headed back to Baltimore, but the pears were finally in New York. But running overlength and overweight was a headache, especially because Red and Dan disliked being illegal. Circumstances had handed us the run; the pears had to get delivered, Dan was the only possibility, and he needed the work. "You do what you have to do," is the attitude. Most discouraging was that by the time all the fines were paid not much profit would be left. To put it mildly.

Based on my experiences, it is much easier to run legal. On the other hand, independents like Ike argue that it is better to learn the habits of the hunters, load heavy for the extra revenue, and head for the "bushes" when necessary. Or, like Jack, the independent can run the turnpikes through Pennsylvania, Ohio, and Indiana paying by weight and not worrying about scales. But then, of course, there are the tolls.

One way or the other independents have to deal with the web of regulations and the various officials who enforce them. With the force of authority behind them, the officials are in control and harassment is always a possibility. But whether the independent chooses to run legally or illegally through the interstate maze, the trip depends on the truck. If it quits, so does he. And unless he is a mechanic with a shop in his trailer, truck problems bring him into a new set of dependency relationships.

Chapter 10

Road
Repairs

Mechanical Problems

The perfect truck, unfortunately, has not yet been manufactured. An independent will run his truck about a hundred thousand miles a year—or he had better if he wants to make a living. (The ICC survey reported an average of ninety-one thousand miles.) The truck will travel over increasingly deteriorating highways at high speeds, often pulling eighty thousand pounds of weight. "Gentle" is not a term usually associated with truckers, but on several occasions that is exactly the term they used to describe the proper way to treat a truck. Even with the best treatment, though, breakdowns occur.

When they do, someone has to repair the truck. The independents that I have interviewed, and others that I have met, vary in mechanical ability. At one extreme are those who barely touch the truck; they only do basic maintenance, if that. At the other are those who are qualified mechanics. Cal emphasized that mechanical ability is critical for an aspiring independent; without it he will acquire many revenue-consuming expenses.

Cal and Irv had the good fortune to be trained as mechanics before they went into trucking. Cal told a story about his brother to emphasize his point about the importance of mechanical savvy:

One of the biggest things today with an owner/operator, if you can't do the biggest part of your work, you might as well forget it. If you can't take care of your equipment, the biggest part of it, you may as well forget it. I'm facing that problem right now with friends of mine around here. They use my garage out here a lot and all. In fact one of them just came to me in the past week. Forty-seven hundred dollars he spent on the truck in the past year and it's not worth a damn right now. And he's taking it back again. And this is what's breaking him. The repair bills is breaking him. I was fortunate enough that—well, everybody says I'm one of a hundred. I can overhaul a diesel motor, a transmission, or a gas motor. Anything I want to overhaul I can overhaul it. (You can do it yourself, huh? Well, the way shop costs are going I guess that would be pretty critical.) That's what I say. If you can't—today where we used to pay a dollar and a half-two dollars-three dollars to get a tire changed, today it's ten-fifteen dollars. And price of fuel and everything, you just got to cut corners wherever you can cut it, that's all. And if a man isn't willing to go out there and work and hustle you can't—there's too many fellows that's starting out that thinks this thing is a white-glove job, that you just go out there and crawl in the truck and drive. You can't do it.

I have a brother that started out two years ago, and I got him started as an owner/operator. 'Fact, I got him his job. Went around with him to help him get the truck. Got him straightened out. He's starting to understand a little, but he was one of them that believed that you just crawl in the truck and go. [story about illness deleted] He's been a truck driver all his life, on and off, but he was never what you really call an owner/operator. And I told him, two years ago when he was getting into this thing, I said, "I'll tell you right now it's going to be a hard problem because you don't know it. You don't understand it. You don't know the racket. You're going to have to learn it. I'll do everything I can to teach you and tell you."

Well, right off the reel he thought you just crawled into a truck, and you started running wherever you go, till the motor blew up one day. No money to fix the motor. And he has it in his head you go up and down the road seventy–seventy-five miles an hour, seventy mile an hour, overrunning the governor and all. You can do this once in a while, but it catches up with you, and this is what happened. He wound her out over the governor one night and throwed the rods out of it and everything. Got the truck fixed up, put him in debt a lot of money. He took it right out and done the same thing right over. And I tried to tell him at that time that he was going to have to back off. The truck wasn't made to run like—it wasn't an automobile.

After teaching us about the importance of mechanical ability, Cal talks about his brother, who began his career without much mechanical sense. It sounds like the brother is learning, but the hard and expensive way. (The description of overrunning the governor should make you skeptical when you hear about monster trucks breaking the speed limit; some do, but if they are pushed too hard and too long they self-destruct.)

Throwing the rods is extreme although in the following trip descriptions it sounds almost typical. But independent after independent, like Ike, often talks about how some annoying mechanical problem usually occurs on a trip, with a price tag and a time delay attached.

I have had good trips and had some bad ones, but I never did actually have just actually a good trip. There's always going to be some problem somewhere along the line in trucking, because you're going to have flat tires, little small minor repair bills, or something. So you can say you be lucky if you make a trip and you don't have no problems at all. That's even with a new truck. You buy a new truck today and you go out with it. Within three to four weeks or months you going to have to buy something minor to go on that in order to complete your trip or journey or something. It just ain't there. They don't build the trucks they used to build.

The unusual trip is without some kind of problem, even if only minor. In the following story Dan describes road repair problems, but does conclude that this trip was not typical:

We hauled a load from L.A. up to Montana. And it was just a bad deal all the way from the start. Loading, getting up there, you know, blowing tires, crap like that. Three-day drive, it takes you about six days to get up there because of all the trouble you're having. It just, you know, you just had a bad deal. Like on that trip there I think I blew about four or five tires. I'm not sure. But it was just a bad trailer. I was pulling company trailers at the time. Just bad, that's all there was to it, you know. Everything went wrong, that's all. It happens every once in a while, trips like that happen.

Mechanical problems are normal; they will happen, and when they do, they cost in delays and expenses. As in every other area of trucking, inflation has not helped. Carl illustrates with a story about the good old days:

(What do you think the major changes are, say, between when you started trucking and now? The good and the bad.) Ain't nothing good now. (It's all bad, huh?) It's all bad. I mean repairs are too much. You go to a stupid truck stop where a guy don't know his ass from his elbow, and they want thirty dollars an hour. You know, and to go into a company like the White company or the Ford company or something like that. They're not going to fix it. They're going to replace it. You know, you can't hate them, because they got to guarantee it. But there's a lot of stuff that can be fixed. Don't have to replace it. So if you pull in and tell them to fix it, Christ, it'll cost you eighty-seven thousand dollars.

See, years ago you didn't have that problem. My exhaust system broke one time. I forget where I was. Man, I was in Boonieboonie, Alabama. And the dang exhaust came right out of the manifold, you know, with the gas job. And like to choke me to death driving, you know. So I finally come up on a gas station. I said, "Man, where can I get some welding done?" "You go down back the road there for three or four miles, and you'll see a telegraph pole. And you make a right-hand turn. There's a big barn back there, and old Jed he's a pretty good old welder, see." So down I go, you know, and pull into this barn. And here's an old guy in there's got a 1918 setup. Got a lathe going. You know what spinning on a lathe is. Like making vases and stuff like that. Ain't too many people can do that. So he come over looked at the truck. Says, "Shucks, that ain't nothing," you know. Two minutes, whole job's done. I'm on my way.

But you can't do that nowadays. There ain't too many down-homers. Everybody's all commercialized. They don't want to even look at you unless you got a hundred dollar bill. Everything you get done costs you a hundred bucks. So you know, there's just too damn much pressure out there. And like I say, with everything so high and the damn rates, you know, for freight are so low. Just can't say nothing good.

Most independents are not mechanics, breakdowns are inevitable, and costs of repairs have gone up along with everything else in recent years. Those premises themselves lead to unfortunate conclusions. When road problems come up the independent is away from his home base, where he knows the good prices and reliable mechanics. He has to get the problem fixed quickly, and everyone he deals with knows that. He is, in short, at the mercy of whomever he happens to find. Following is a story on this theme that I told to Steve and Dave and their reactions to it:

(I was talking to this guy I was telling you about before.)
Steve: Yeah, I don't know who that could be. That name doesn't ring a bell.
(I may have his last name wrong, Steve, 'cause I just met him at the independent thing—the meeting there. But he invited me over to his house and said, "Well, I want to show you how a trip works." And he pulled out all his papers and stuff. On this particular trip he was driving to Texas, and his alternator was acting goofy. So he pulled up to this shop in some little town and this guy gave him this line of stuff and fixed it. Gave him a receipt for 130 bucks, right? Gets a couple of miles down the road, alternator starts acting goofy again. And he finally went a few more miles and he pulled in to another spot. Guy looked at it. You know what it was? It was the condenser that was on the alternator to keep the noise down for the CB. Took the guy two and a half seconds to fix it. Charged him 15 bucks or something. Other guy back up the road got him for 130 bucks.)
Steve: You're at the mercy [all talk at once].
Dave: When you're on the road, they know that you're away from home. They know that you got to go. And whatever you want you

Independents Declared

can betcha it's going to cost you three times as much as if you were home.

Steve: Mike, you would have got a kick out of the old guy that used to work with us out of Cleveland. He was still driving when he was about seventy years old. And he'd been born in Germany and never lost much of his accent. His v's and w's got all mixed up. He was one of the guys that made money. Don't ask me how he did it, but he made it good. But he used to say, "Ven you plunk your ass down behind that veel, you become a hunted animal." And that is exactly what you become. You're fair game for every badge-toter out there, for every alley garage or wrecker or jackleg mechanic. And eventually you're going to have to do it, because you break down somewhere out in west nowhere, and you got to rely on this guy. Because you don't have a burn torch with you. You don't have a special wrench to fit a nut that's that big or something like that. And then you're at their mercy.

The story that I recounted (and had seen the receipts from) shows how road repairs may lead to exploitation of an independent by unscrupulous mechanics. Steve's and Dave's reactions suggest that for them the story is not unusual. Here is another example, from a series of similar stories told by Will:

I give you an example. I blew a tire in New Jersey. I'm honest, see. I could have called in and said, "Hey, I blew a tire on the trailer," and it was actually on my tractor, and had the company buy me—but my mind don't work that way. Until I have a problem, and then if a company seduces me, then I feel that I must do it back or do something. You know, basically I try to be honest. So I had a flat tire in New Jersey. I went in the diner. I know for a fact that two miles down the road there's a place that fixes tires. And I also know they have a twenty-four-hour number. So I stopped in the diner because I know they're closed. Ain't no sense going down there and sitting there. Got a cup of coffee. I called the company and told them. They give me the man's night number. I called the guy, and I said, "Pal, I'm only two miles from your place." I said, "I'll meet you down there. I'll be down there about five or ten minutes." I said, "That way I'm saving a road service call, right?"

I started to walk across the road, and as I got to my truck, here comes the guy with the tire truck pulling in alongside of my truck. I said, "Hey, I told you I was going to meet you down the shop there." He says, "Well, you ain't that far away." He says, "I figured I'd just come on up here." I said, "Well, you know that I'm not paying no road service call." He said, "Oh, well, I got to charge you road service." I says, "Like hell you will." I says, "I told you I'd meet you in front of your damn shop." He said, "Alright. Then we'll go down to the shop." I said O.K. We drove down to the shop.

I told the guy, I said, "I'd like to get"—I'm only about 140 miles from home, which I have tires in my yard. I said, "What I'd like to do is I get a used tire and put it on just enough to get me home." "Oh, I don't think we have any used tires," he says. "You have to get a brand new tire." I said, "Well, how much is that." "It's 280 dollars." I said, "Hey pal, do me a favor. Take the tire off. Put the rim back on." I says, "I'll run down the goddamn road like that." Which is really illegal with a loaded trailer. "No, wait a minute," he says. "I remember. Yeah, that's right. We do have—I got one used tire." He says, "That's all I got's one used tire." Hundred and fifteen dollars it cost me. I mean now, I suppose on that load I probably made fifty dollars if I made that much after tolls. That's on a one-way side. Over the whole thing I might have made more.

You can't blame the mechanic for trying to earn a living, especially since Will's call sounds like it came at an inconvenient hour. But still, the story shows Will's vulnerability. He avoided the forced sale only by refusing service and threatening to drive home on one tire. He had an alternative to his dependence on the road mechanic.

From these accounts, it is clear that mechanical problems on the road are to be expected, that they will delay the trip (when you're not moving you're not making money), and that they will add to expenses. Sometimes a major breakdown (like the type that Cal described earlier, or that Irv and others talk about) will put the independent right out of business. When they occur, he will probably need the help of a mechanic or other repairman. Alongside the highway with a vanload of freight, he can only hope for honesty. Breakdowns turn him into a turtle lying on its back. He just hopes the person who comes along will flip him over rather than using him for soup.

Breakdowns on the Trips

During my three long trips, mechanical problems always occurred. So serious were the major problems that I will not detail the minor ones like lights, filters, tires, and side-windows. The worst disaster occurred on the trip with Red. We were running on a two-lane highway in the middle of some beautiful isolated western nowhere. It was the first time, in my judgment, that Red was pushing himself too hard. His style was to rest around nine or ten at night, then get up around two or three in the morning, have breakfast, and leave.

It was around midnight with over a hundred miles to go. Red had not planned to be driving so long. He was in what for him was new territory; he had asked at a truck stop and two cafes about the highway and the conditions to expect. We were told, at the last stop, that two long "pulls" lay ahead of us and then flat and clean road all the way to Winnemucca.

They lied or they must not have known the road or the current conditions. We encountered hill after hill, which takes time with the small Cummins 290 engine that was in Red's truck. Ice patches scattered unpredictably here and there further slowed us. The strain showed, because it was the first and only time that Red told me, very politely, to shut up while he concentrated on driving.

As we crested one hill, we saw another eighteen-wheeler parked halfway up the next. We tried to call him on the CB but did not get an answer. Red stopped on top of the hill looking for some signal. He worried about pulling up alongside the other truck in the middle of another hill; with the small engine, getting started again with a loan would be difficult. But that is what we eventually had to do.

The driver of the parked truck was also an independent, team-driving with his wife. Going up the hill, she noticed the water temperature moving toward boiling, pulled over to avoid overheating the engine, and woke him up. The amazing thing, to me, was that Red and the other driver started talking like they were having coffee in a truck stop. "How you doing?" "Where you out of?" "What you got on?" and so on.

The truck's fan clutch was not working. A fan clutch turns off the engine cooling fan when the temperature is below a certain limit—it saves the engine from working unnecessarily to drive the fan when the engine is cool anyway. Unfortunately, the clutch stayed off even after the temperature went up. The independent was packing snow into the radiator to cool it down. We jury-rigged a melting pot, built a fire to get more water, and helped him pack snow into the radiator. After about half an hour, another truck came along and stopped. That driver, a former independent now driving for a company, looked at the engine, got some tools, and rigged the fan clutch so that it was permanently engaged. That cooled the engine and we drove off convoy style toward Winnemucca.

The company driver was a local, so he led the way and provided navigational instructions on the CB. "Watch this hill because there's a 45 mph curve at the bottom and the sign means it." He also entertained us with some local lore that I would have preferred not to have heard. "On your right is about a thousand foot drop. Guy parked his rig there to take a leak, forgot to set the brake, and the damn thing went right over the side. Still sits down there at the bottom." Because the local driver's and the other independent's engines were bigger, they eventually pulled ahead, although we had them in sight.

We came to a T-intersection, stopped, and turned south toward Winnemucca. With a sickening noise the cab began to vibrate and the engine to lose power. We pulled to the side of the road as the

Cummins shuddered and died. Red, exhausted, slumped over the steering wheel for a moment, then looked at me and said something like "this is really it." I was already beginning to feel like a vegetarian at a bullfight; to see economic ruin come from nowhere and strike someone I liked and respected was more powerful than I can convey.

Red called for help on the CB and the other two trucks came back. While we waited he pulled himself together, set out the emergency reflectors, and began checking the reefer to be sure the unit was still operating. The local driver returned first, and after some discussion it was decided that I would ride with him into Winnemucca—a hundred miles distant—and find a towtruck. Red would stay with the load, arguing that he would know what to do if the refrigeration unit malfunctioned. We left him with a can of coke, a bag of cookies, and an extra blanket provided by the local driver, and headed for town.

As we began our trip, I explained to the local driver that I was a professor doing research with independents. He said, "You are? Well, I started trucking in. . . ." It was as if he had driven around for years waiting to be interviewed. Considering my feelings at the time, it was the ultimate in irony. Research was the farthest thing from my mind. He was an interesting man, but eventually we stopped talking and I dozed off. Though I had only been a passenger, we had left Portland in the early morning, gone to Medford for the pears, and been on the road since. Besides, while Red slept, I had done some chores—supplies, laundry, and notes. "Every truck needs an anthropologist" was the joke on that trip.

When we got to town around 3:00 a.m., I went into the truck stop and called the twenty-four-hour towing number posted on the board. Later I learned that Jim, the towtruck driver, had just gotten back from hauling another vehicle in from the desert. The local driver waited to make sure everything was O.K., and then decided to accept my offer to buy him breakfast. In the truck stop we saw the other independent, and I received one of my all-time favorite left-handed compliments. They asked me questions about what I was doing and why, and the local driver finally said he wished that some of the "other assholes" would get out on the road and see what it was like.

Ultimately, Jim showed up and we rode back out to Red and the truck. The engine failure was diagnosed as a cracked crankshaft and the truck eventually had to be towed to Reno for repairs. The towing bill (including the trip to Reno) was $750; I later learned that the engine repair was $4,500, most of which had to be financed. After much telephoning and considering of alternatives, we eventually put the trailer onto Dan's tractor and, a couple of days late, delivered the load to New York City. The trip, obviously, was a total disaster.

To balance this worst-case story is an account of a road repair on my trip with Ike. Early in the trip we stopped for him to tinker with the refrigeration unit. He was carrying a load of meat in the van, and the unit was not keeping the temperature low enough. By bypassing the thermostat he got the temperature low enough to finish the delivery in Pennsylvania. Next we hauled dry freight to Texas and did not need the reefer. But in the Valley we picked up a load of cabbage and had to get the unit functioning properly. Ike had a directory of twenty-four-hour reefer repair locations, and on Saturday night we called a service man in Tennessee. He and his daughter met us in a parking lot and guided us to his garage.

He worked on the unit for about two hours. He found that he needed a valve he did not have in stock, so he jury-rigged the unit to work until Ike got home. No charge. He said that since he didn't fix it, he couldn't charge. This is a striking counterexample to the stories of getting robbed on the road by unscrupulous mechanics. As we headed toward Virginia and home, Ike said he was going to try to figure a way to go back there for the repair to give the man his business.

The next story falls between Red's devastating experience and Ike's ordinary breakdown. Jack pulled up to the gate of the steel plant near Chicago to get his load. The security guard said that only one driver was allowed into the plant, and despite our attempt to convince him that the "co-driver" should go in, he held to the company rules. I was dropped at the drivers' waiting room—a small stone building with a rough wooden bench and a couple of office chairs with torn vinyl and escaping springs. The walls were yellow tile streaked with grime, and a broken window was stuffed with wadded-up newspaper. I asked a guard in the nearby station if I could get a cup of coffee. With a curt "no" he went back to his telephone. Although by now I knew that most drivers' areas ranged from spartan to downright insulting, this one topped—or rather bottomed—them all.

After about an hour, the female half of a husband-wife team came in and we started to wisecrack about the beauty of the place when a guard came in and gave me a number to call. As I picked up the phone, the captain was talking about some guy's battery blowing up. The guy was Jack. On the phone Jack told me to get into the loading area to help him. I made my request three times, up the local heirarchy back to the captain. All three said "what are you going to do for him?" to which I always said with genuine exasperation that my partner's truck broke down and I needed to help him work on it. Finally the captain drove me in.

Jack had been told to back into and out of a loading door several times. The last time the truck's starter wouldn't turn over, so the crane operator gave him a push. As the engine turned over one of the four batteries exploded and the starter caught on fire. When I arrived the cab was jacked up and the damage was obvious by both sight and smell. Fortunately, the crew were considerate people. One of them said he knew "how it is." They let us park and work on the truck there, and told us not to worry—the load would be ready when we were. They showed us the coffee pot, telephone, and bathroom and went back to their work.

Fortunately we had gotten to know a fine dispatcher, a woman whose late husband had been a driver. Jack called her and she recommended a road mechanic. We called the mechanic, his wife paged him on the beeper, and he arrived within an hour. He rewired the truck onto two batteries, saying that would be enough to run the electrical equipment. Then he taped the offending starter wires, gave us a tow, and got us started. All we had to do then was not let the engine die until we got back to Baltimore where Jack could get a new battery and have the starter rebuilt. The mechanic was a former independent; he charged only eighty-five dollars for the road visit and the repair work.

Jack backed in again and the crane started dropping steel beams onto the flatbed trailer. I stayed with the loaders to make sure that there was room to put up the sides when they were done. Jack went to the bathroom, came back, and walked around the truck, and suddenly began swearing as he shut off the engine. A pool of oil was forming under the truck. Jack sent me to call the mechanic again; he came back when the loading was nearly finished. The problem was that the starter wire shorting had put a chink in the high-pressure hose that went from the engine to the sending unit for the oil pressure gauge in the cab. After the engine started, the chink eventually opened up and started pumping oil out onto the floor. The mechanic pulled the hose out and put a bolt into the hole. Jack was going to have to run without an oil pressure gauge, though he would still have the warning light. The mechanic said he hated to do it, but he had to charge us something. It came to an additional fifty dollars, which Jack had to borrow from me since he had run out of cash. Finally, at midnight rather than 5:00 p.m., we chained down the load, put the sides up, tied on the tarp, and limped onto the interstate and back toward the East.

From the trips I learned several things. Though both Red and Jack told me that my experiences with them were not typical, major breakdowns occur with some regularity. The damage in time and money—not to mention personal strain—was substantial. To get the idea, imagine yourself facing an unexpected event with unknown consequences in a strange place, an event that has the potential of ruining you economically. Second, I learned that when faced with road repairs the independent wants to do the minimum necessary to complete the run; when he gets home he can do his own work or use familiar people and suppliers. Third, I learned that the mechanics we dealt with, who did indeed have us completely at their mercy, ran from decent and honest to downright generous. I have heard many other stories about road robbery, but on my trips road generosity was more the case. As in many other areas of the interviews, reality typically was not as bad as the stories suggest, a difference that will be explored in the next chapter.

Chapter 11

Independence

The Cultural Image

By now the "independent" in "independent trucker" should seem to be a misnomer. In story after story independents talk about themselves as embedded in business and regulatory systems with surprisingly little personal control over choices or outcomes. "Dependent trucker" might be a more appropriate phrase.

The irony is that independent truckers are romanticized in novels, movies, and television as mythic American heroes—the last of the cowboys, the sole surviving heirs of the American ideal of unrestrained personal freedom. By now it should be clear why independents resent these popularizations. Popular novels like *Convoy* have little to do with the reality of an independent's working world. An examination of *Convoy* and another popular novel of the same genre, *The Last of the Cowboys*, will help clarify the differences between them and the many stories in this book.

In the *The Last of the Cowboys* by Max Franklin, an independent trucker with the handle of "Elegant John" lies dying in a Los Angeles hospital. He is called "elegant" because, "When you drive a couple of million miles, and you never get a ticket, or a blowout, and you never lose a day in the shops, and you're always on time, then that's elegant" (1977:34). (It is also impossible, but never mind.) With the help of his roommate, John escapes from the hospital. Although his truck (named "Eleanor" after Eleanor Roosevelt) has been repossessed, he breaks in to the lot and "steals it back." All he wants, in his last few days, is to make a "perfect run" from one coast to the other.

The book is the story of Elegant John's last trip. He first picks up a strange young bible-quoting man, named Beebo, who is on his way to Florida to attend motel management school. Then he drives to Idaho, because he heard that a load of refrigerators was available.

150   *Independents Declared*

The load is refused because the shipper finds out that the truck is stolen. John drives to a little town in Wyoming, where a woman friend runs a house of prostitution that caters to truckers. The prostitutes have been ordered to leave town by the court, so they strike a deal with Elegant John to pay expenses of the trip, put their belongings and themselves in the trailer, and head for South Carolina to begin anew.

This unlikely crew heads east. They are arrested and then escape from two ignorant police officers who operate a speed trap in a small Missouri town. In Georgia they pull in to a truck stop as the television newscaster wishes them luck on the "last perfect run." News coverage has built up to the point where they are now national heroes; the patrons of the truck stop cheer them at the end of the news spot.

Meanwhile, an evil trucker, Charlie by name, keeps appearing and causing trouble; he wants Elegant John arrested so he can buy his truck cheap. Charlie informs the Georgia state police of Elegant John's backroad route, and they—with little enthusiasm at the prospect of arresting a national hero—set up a roadblock at a bridge. Leading a convoy made up of trucks and a group of local citizens in cars and vans, Elegant John runs the blockade and heads for South Carolina. Although the state police now leave him alone, Elegant John dies only twenty miles from Hilton Head, so Beebo drives them in. He and the prostitutes bury Elegant John on the seacoast, sing his favorite song, and then drive off.

In *Convoy*, by B.W.L. Norton, the hero is an independent trucker with the CB handle of "Rubber Duck." As he drives down an Arizona highway, Duck meets Melissa, a wealthy journalist, when he is forced to deal with her erratic driving. He then contends with two policemen in succession, one an easily distracted fool and the other, named Lyle, an old-time pro at harassment of truckers. After all of this opening highway action, he finally gets to a truck stop. Lyle appears, and eventually the situation develops to the point where Lyle harasses another trucker and Duck knocks him out. Duck and several other truckers form into a convoy and run for the New Mexico border to escape arrest. Melissa, who came to the truck stop after her car broke down, stows away in Duck's truck. Duck jilts the waitress he usually sleeps with, and she gets even by waking up Lyle who sets off after the convoy.

Using back roads and outwitting Lyle and other police, the convoy makes it to the state line. More and more trucks join, so that by the time they enter New Mexico (running by a scale in the process) they are twenty. Now the FBI enters the picture, and in coordination with Lyle they set up a roadblock. Duck points out on the CB that he is hauling Class B explosives, so the roadblock is hastily removed. As they roll along through a small New Mexico town under police escort, Duck explains the situation to Melissa: "'This here convoy,' he concluded, indicating it with a sweep of his hand toward the mirror, is maybe our way of sayin' we're here, too. And we got to be counted a little more often'" (1978:84).

By now the media coverage is extensive, and this in turn leads to more trucks joining the convoy. A news van pulls up next to Duck, and with Melissa's prompting, he says, "Yeah, we're headin' right up to Washington, D.C. The way I see it, it's the workingman against all that government red tape and stupidity ... (1978:89). Public support grows. The governor of New Mexico sets up a meeting in a park. Meanwhile Lyle is stumbling through a series of encounters and generally making a fool of himself.

After they arrive at the park, one of the truckers heads home because his wife is about to give birth. When he gets to Texas, he is waylaid and beaten up by Lyle and the local truck-hating police officer. The story is passed along from CB to CB up to New Mexico. Duck, who is just concluding a successful conference with the governor, takes off for Texas. Several others follow him even though he tells them to take advantage of their newly won amnesty. The seven truckers run through the small Texas town, beat up Lyle and the other officer, and then separate again.

Now the largest convoy of all forms, but in short order the truckers see that traps have been set and they split up. Duck and a few others turn south to hide out in Mexico. The Texas governor has called out the National Guard, and they have set up a blockade at a bridge. The trucks stop, but Duck finally squeezes past a tank and heads across the bridge. Lyle gets his hands on a machine gun and fires at Duck's trailer until the explosives go off.

Duck becomes a hero; national campaigns start to repeal the 55-mile-per-hour speed limit and investigate the oil companies. Then the happy ending—it turns out that the reason Duck's body was never found is that he landed in the river and lived. He finds Melissa, and they sneak away from his funeral for parts unknown.

In these novels the independent trucker protagonists move through situations with a quiet self-reliance. Governmental representatives, especially police, challenge their independence by trying to control them, often as an exercise in the use of brute authority rather than as a means to some reasonable end. And institutional authority is often portrayed as corrupting, since it is sometimes drawn from, parasite-like, to accomplish base personal ends.

In the conflict between independence and control, independence enjoys the moral advantage. The popular support for both protagonists is overwhelming, facilitated in both cases by media attention. And in the final confrontations, over blockades on backroad bridges, with the forces of the state dramatically arrayed before them, high-level state representatives express ambivalence about their controlling action. After the protagonists conquer the blockades, both disappear; one dies; the other, thought dead by others, disappears in disguise into a hidden and unknown future. What else can they do after a successful, defiant display of independence? They can never return to ordinary daily life, for their return, as we all know too well, would immediately contradict their achievement. The only honorable exit with their heroic status intact is disappearance.

To begin to understand the myth of the independent trucker it is helpful to compare the two novels with a real story told by Steve and Dave. The details of the story and the kinds of problems described are familiar, but it compresses and dramatizes in one story many of the problems that can occur with various carriers on many trips, and is thus parallel to the compressed action of a novel.

An independent named Bill learns that his two-year-old child is very sick at home in Sioux City. Bill, located in Buffalo at this time, looks for a load going west but cannot find one. Coldfreight Trucking has a load going to Boston, and offers to load him from Boston to Great Falls, Montana. Bill pulls the load to Boston and finds that his trailer does not have enough cubic footage to carry the Montana freight. (Bill's trailer is a "twelve-foot-six-inch high forty-footer with rails in it"; refrigerated vans can be higher and longer, and one without "rails" along the ceiling for "swinging meat" could carry more.)

Bill has to rent a trailer from Coldfreight at a cost of twenty-five dollars a day. The company offers not to charge him for the weekend days. He eventually gets home and spends a couple of days with his child, then leaves to unload in Montana and find another load to get him back East. His tractor catches on fire in Wyoming, burning up the wiring and the air hoses. A wrecker tows him the sixty miles to Rawlins for three hundred dollars. He gets new air lines and runs some wiring from the small diesel that runs the refrigeration unit on the trailer to provide electricity for the truck.

At this point Bill has a load of potatoes that he picked up in Idaho due in Cleveland the next day, but no money. He tries to get an advance from the broker who arranged the load, but is refused. He then tries Coldfreight, but it will not put up money for another carrier's load. He argues with the Coldfreight dispatcher, pointing out that he has money due him for loads already delivered for Cold-freight that would serve as security against an advance. He does not persuade Coldfreight and finally the broker gives him some cash.

At this point it is helpful to review the many facts about trucking from past chapters that are condensed in the story so far. Bill is permanently leased to Coldfreight Trucking. It loads him first to Boston and then to Montana carrying its freight, using its authority. It also rents him a company trailer, since the one he owns is too small. Once he gets in the West, though, Coldfreight does not have the authority to give him freight to come back. Bill contacts a "broker"—someone who pairs up trucks with agricultural loads. Since unprocessed agricultural goods are exempt, Bill can load potatoes into the van and carry them without worrying about ICC authority.

When an independent gets a load, he also gets an "advance"—money he can use to buy fuel and food for the trip. The advance is then deducted from his settlement sheet when he is paid for the trip. When Bill calls Coldfreight for an advance, it refuses him because he is not carrying its freight. Bill argues that there are enough checks due him from past trips, in various stages of preparation in the company offices, to secure the advance. I do not understand why the broker who set up the load of potatoes refused to advance Bill initially but later agreed. Perhaps Dave, the storyteller, did not know or could not remember what really happened and tacked that fact on to continue the story.

Bill drives on, but then has problems with one of the wheels. That eats up his advance money so he calls his wife to get more cash for the trip. When he runs out of that money, he calls the broker and the Coldfreight dispatcher and finally gets enough money to get to Cleveland and unload the potatoes, though he is now a few days late. The customer could file a claim against him for the delay but the story does not state whether this happened. Bill retrieves his own trailer and eventually returns to Sioux City ready to settle for "the round"—all the trips taken since he originally left. Between the advances and the trailer rental, including the weekend rent that he was told would not be charged, he owes Coldfreight money. He tells the dispatcher to pay it with his license account.

This "license account" is maintained by Coldfreight as Bill's permanent lease carrier, to be sure at the end of the year the "base plate" (home state license plate) fee is covered. Because Bill is broke and discouraged at the end of this round and does not expect to be with the carrier for another year he tells Coldfreight to take the money owed out of his license account. As Steve said at this part of the story, "if he didn't have bad luck he wouldn't have had any luck."

Now Bill is disgusted with Coldfreight and starts the process of leasing on with a new carrier—Swensen. In the interim he drives a friend's truck. The Coldfreight dispatcher hears Bill is driving and assumes he has leased with Swensen. This would be illegal, since an independent can permanent lease to only one carrier at a time. So the Coldfreight dispatcher calls Swensen, and Swensen stops Bill's paperwork. But Bill is doing nothing wrong; he is driving someone else's truck, not the one that is leased to Coldfreight. In disgust Bill goes to the dispatcher, takes off the plates and company identification signs that go on the tractor door, and demands the return of his license fee. He has to argue to get Coldfreight to process this work in time for a refund. As Dave wraps it up, ". . . he just got screwed from about three different ends at one time, and you know there ain't but two ends to anything." Unlike Elegant John and Rubber Duck, Bill is losing his battles with institutional authority. His story more accurately summarizes the themes of independent trucking expressed in the stories in this book.

So how did Rubber Duck and Elegant John come about? The novels make three crucial simplifications. First, real stories show that a trip for an independent goes like this: get a load, load it, make the trip, unload it, get paid. Problems can come up anywhere along the line. But in the novels, almost everything is left out but the trip. In fact, the only loading occurs when Elegant John "hears about" some refrigerators in Idaho; he drives up from southern Nevada and sure enough, there they are. The novel does not intend to be realistic, but that is sheer nonsense.

The second simplification is that the trips are not realistic or typical but rather are of a special sort. The purpose is not to deliver freight; instead, it is to make the last perfect run or to avoid arrest. One of the protagonists in *Convoy* has a load of live hogs, obviously for entertainment value, but one cannot help wondering who is taking care of them and how large the independent's liability will be for them, since the rules of the game are that once the freight's on your truck it's your responsibility. In the fictional trips, trucks never break down, even after crashing through blockades, tearing up trees in a town park, and taking out the front wall of a jailhouse. No one sleeps often or buys much fuel, and when they do two hundred gallons comes awfully cheap.

The novels make a third crucial simplification; nothing describes how an independent gets into business in the first place. He has to purchase a tractor and perhaps a trailer (the two together currently moving toward a new price of a hundred thousand dollars), pick a carrier to lease on with, and manage to stay in business in a service industry with high operating costs, one of the most vulnerable to business failure. Further, he has to do this on rates that are among the lowest in the trucking industry (and getting lower all the time under deregulation) while at the same time assuming all costs of truck, salary, and trip expenses.

To sum all this up, the stories *about* independent truckers, as told by and for nontruckers, leave out most of the details of the working world that are significant *to* independent truckers when they tell stories about each other. When independents talk about trucking, they tell stories that illustrate the theme of dependence— the trucker depends on carriers for loads, paperwork, and payment; on mechanics for road repairs; on company employees for loading and unloading; on regulatory officials to check a number of things about him, his truck, and his freight.

The fact that fiction and reality are different is obvious, but what do the differences show about the cultural use of independent truckers? First, *The Last of the Cowboys* and *Convoy* are stories told about members of a group, but by and to nonmembers. On the other hand, the story of Bill is told about an independent (Bill) by an independent (Dave) to an independent (Steve). The novels celebrate independents as personifications of traditional American values of individual freedom and self-reliance. But the story about Bill, a summary of many of the themes in the preceding chapters, describes their working world as a series of dependency relationships in which they are powerless. If cultural tradition and social encounter can be thought of as two different "message sources," then independents are boxed into a paradox. They carry the popular cultural image of independence, but their working world is full of reminders that others are in control.

Another interesting difference between fiction and reality lies in the type of institution that causes the independent's problems. Though the hospital and the bank are the first antagonists of *The Last of the Cowboys*, by and large the two novels emphasize the state as the controlling institution. In the story of Bill, on the other hand, problems were caused by carriers, brokers, and mechanics. Though government authorities do play a role in some of the independent's stories, and though government policy sets up the conditions in the first place, much in the interviews identifies fellow occupants of the private sector as major sources of dependency.

Other aspects of the independent's life as described in the interviews are different from fiction. For example, everyone in the novels uses CB handles; the interviews barely mention them. Elegant John and Rubber Duck are alone in the world; Bill has a wife and sick child at home, and in his story we glimpse the frequent role of the wife as keeper of the books (and probably earner of a second income) as prevalent in the interviews. But these differences will not be explored now.

My first contact with independents, at a meeting in Baltimore in late 1981, led to an invitation to describe what I was trying to do. I talked about research, explained my interest in the topics of small business and regulation, and said I would like to interview people about their careers in trucking and go on some trips. The reaction was a general discussion, involving most of those at the meeting, about how the research I was describing was a good idea because there were so many unrealistic portrayals of independent trucking in the popular media. An independent's wife commented that movies and television gave the idea that trucking is just riding down the road, and an independent wisecracked that he had not seen any of them unload yet.

The subject of movies and television came up in interviews on occasion, as in this excerpt from Steve and Dave.

> Dave: You know that's just about like—here back awhile I was reading in *Overdrive*. This driver was talking to this TV fellow about, you know, they got like *BJ and the Bear*.
> Steve: Hasn't helped the industry any.
> Dave: Let's see, what was that other one that was on there that had . . .
> Steve: *Sonny and Will*.
> Dave: Yeah.
> Steve: *Moving On*.
> Dave: *Moving On*, and all them. He says, "You know, you watch one of these shows and you get this conception about what it's like to go truck driving that's just totally unreal. Why don't you put something on there about the actual events that a trucker goes through in a day?" And so they went out and they'd go, you know. He's going around this and that and the other. And they get it all done and they ask him what he thinks of it. And he says, "Yeah, that's pretty good." He says, "You going to run it?" "No."
> Steve: Nobody'd ever believe it.
> Dave: Says, "Why not?" "Nobody'd ever believe it."

One of my favorite stories on the topic was told to me in a truck stop near Baltimore. Apparently a reporter walked into the truck stop, announced that he wanted to talk to independent truckers, and sat at a table with several of them. They talked for some time about many of the same issues reported in this study. Suddenly, into the truck stop swaggered an independent decked out in cowboy boots and feathered hat, swearing loudly about one thing and another. The reporter dropped everything, fired up the tape recorder, interviewed him, and left. I do not mean to say that the press is consistently bad; several times independents made a point of giving me news clippings that they found to be fair and accurate. (A good general article appeared in *Parade*, April 30, 1984.) But the reporter I heard about in Baltimore, like many others whose stories I have read or heard about, was helping perpetuate the cultural myth without even knowing it.

The meeting, the interview, and the story about the reporter all illustrate the same point. Some independents fulfill—even play to—the cultural image; in my travels they usually stood out in truck stops because they look so overdone. That image is the one typically represented in the popular media. Like the American cowboy, it represents the culture's use of a social type to make a statement about itself. But the image leaves out some of the most significant characteristics of the independent's working world. The interviews reveal that those characteristics, seen in different stories about several different domains of independent trucking, emphasize his dependency on those who control his job and his trip. Independent truckers are not just contemporary versions of the older, equally inaccurate image of the open-range cowboy; they are small businessmen, independent contractors angered that control over their success is in the hands of so many other people.

Independence

Where is the independence in independent trucking? Perhaps this is why one hears the term "owner/operator" more than "independent." On the other hand, there is something to sitting in the left eye of your eighty-thousand-pound loaded tractor-trailer and watching states roll by, isn't there? Or am I just another nontrucker perpetuating the cultural image that generated *Convoy*? Perhaps analyzing some of the interview material can help clarify this central issue of independence.

When independents talk in summary fashion about their work the contradictions are immediately apparent. Consider these two passages from Jack's interview. First he describes independent trucking in negative terms as he remembers the advice he gave a young man:

> He had a pile of money in his pocket, and he said, "I want to buy a truck and become an owner/operator." And I told him, I says, "You don't want to do it." I said, "You're a goddamn fool." I said, "Don't you do it." I said, "That's the last thing you want to do. You don't want to buy a truck." I said, "It's a dirty, rotten, stinking, lousy—the hardest business that you can get into," which it is.
>
> You know, you're not a human being. You're an animal. You got

everybody and his brother out after you to begin with. You got the DOT. You got the ICC. You got the company. You got company officials. You got the public. You got the police. You got the county police, the state police. You name them and they're all after you. For one reason or another, they're all after you. And every time you go out on that goddamn highway, once you get in that truck you start breaking every law that is put down. And you think you're one of the biggest criminals God ever put on earth. That's the opinion you get after you drive so many years. And everybody thinks you're dirt and filth under their feet. That's the opinion everybody gives you. You're not a human being no more. [skip portion]

Have you ever went down the highway and seen a guy there cutting his grass, and you look at him and you wish to Christ it was you—that you could sit down and do something like that? Many a day I drove past a guy cutting his lawn, seeing him sweating out there. "Man, I wish that was me." I wish I could do something like that. And there you are confined behind that steering wheel, couple thousand miles away from home. That makes you think, you know.

Now compare the harassed, negatively stereotyped independent longing for the settled life, with this passage, which occurred only a few moments later in the same interview:

A lot of time, you like get up in the mountains, you know. Daybreak and stuff like that, you know. And that's when you know ain't nobody as big and as good off and as better off as you are. And the poor son of a bitch slob working in a office, and got to look at them four walls, and I'm looking at the whole United States. The man asked me where I worked at I tell him the East Coast. I don't have to tell him I work in a office or in a factory. I work the East Coast. That's quite a difference there, you know. I'm proud of what I do. I'm proud of what I am. It ain't everybody can do what I can do. I know it. I'm serious over that.

Here's another version of the same contradiction from the interview with Steve.

You can see from the picture over there, I've got quite a few nieces and nephews. And sometimes when they'd be introducing me to their friends, they'd say, "Unc drives a truck," something like that. I'd say, "Play that down. We don't want that to be too well-known we've got a truck driver in the family." Because a lot of the truckers do more or less bring disgrace on themself and on the industry. There's a lot of clowns out there, a lot of cowboys, a lot of them, I'm the first to admit, shouldn't be there. Yet I can show you in the paper that the company puts out each month. We had a guy working here was a graduate of Oxford University in England. I worked with a guy out of Witchita years ago spoke seven languages, spoke and wrote seven languages, including Chinese. He had dropped out of the medical school in Vienna. You will find the whole spectrum in the trucking industry, from the crooks and illiterates up to well-educated people. There's quite a few guys working here that are college graduates. Why they wasted time on a college career to end up trucking is beyond me. One guy, I said, "So what are you doing trucking if you got a college degree?" He says, "I should work for less money just so I can wear a suit and a tie?" Why'd he go to begin with?

(Do you think the independence thing appeals to people still?) I strongly feel that's what draws them to begin with. You find a lot of guys that are owner/operators that are very anti-union, myself for one. There's also the ones that, I guess, were the ones that pushed the frontier back. You know they call the truckers the last American cowboy.

Steve's two uses of the term "cowboy" say it all. The first use, at the beginning of the quote, is current jargon for a flamboyant fool who doesn't take care of business. The second use, at the end, is the trucker as the personification of mythic American frontier independence. Jack and Steve are not the only independents who express this ambivalence. In fact, it appears frequently, though it is not usually as neatly laid out in a short stretch of interview.

Some segments of the interviews that deal with the business are more consistently negative (seldom are they consistently positive). For example, in one segment Irv elaborates on the theme that "you were a truck driver so you was scum." In another segment he talks about how trucking is a bad deal from a business point of view and that "you got more hardships than you got roses in it." The economic pressures are so tough, he continues, that all a young guy will get out of traveling around is—"so what's he going to see, the slums of every city he runs into." (Irv is also the one who talks about other job opportunities—like mechanic and operating engineer—that he wished he had stayed with instead.)

Will is more favorable about trucking. He talks about the enriching experience of learning different styles of living around the United States. Unlike Irv, he praises the traveling (each city has something special to offer, he says); he expresses pride in what he does:

It's amazing to think—you know, I used to enjoy myself. I'd say to my wife or somebody, I'd say, "Man, you know, I'd like to take you out tonight. We'll go to a restaurant in Pittsburgh." And I could be eating lobster at a place called Pete's Restaurant in Pittsburgh. And the next night I could be up in Detroit. There's a little place there that has really great something. And a guy up in Greenwich Village that has the best spaghetti dinners. Up in New Hampshire if you want really good seafood, you know. It's amazing to think that while a guy sleeps ten hours or eight hours during the night I can be in

Chicago, and the next morning I can be in Baltimore. It's really an amazing thing if you think about it. People, I really don't imagine unless they do it would have any concept of it.

Later he says he could "be talking to one guy one day and then be gone a thousand miles and be back two days later and the guy can't imagine what you just did." Cal is also more positive than Irv, expressing pride by describing how trucking requires stamina and mechanical know-how.

I'll say one thing, though. Just everybody can't be a truck driver. Number one, it's got to be something you like, because I've laid out in the snow and the rain and worked on trucks and overhaul transmission—fix tires. You forget about the weather when you got trouble because it's got to be fixed. You got to go. So there's only one thing. Get out there and either fix it because you can't get somebody to fix it half the time. That's the reason I say it takes a special type of a person to be a truck driver.

Alethia (Cal's wife): These young ones don't know what it is, too, like these old ones.

Cal: Number one, you got to be able to get up and go at any hour of the night. You got to be able to go for one or two days without very much rest at a time. Then you got to be able to rest when you get the chance. And there's so many people can't do that.

Endurance is the key, from Cal's point of view. (A quick but relevant aside—I learned about the power of the weather that Cal talks about on the trip with Red. There is something about changing a fuel filter at twenty below zero during the first big winter storm of 1982, or about standing at the top of Lookout Pass in a blizzard talking with other truckers about how many chains to use and which tires to put them on. These stories are not emphasized, but my respect for Mother Nature increased several orders of magnitude because of this research.)

The ambivalence about being an independent trucker continues into discussions about "trying something else." Dan explains why he does not do something else by comparing independent trucking with a job he almost took running a service station:

I've went to school to learn how to operate a service station. Jackson Oil wanted me to go to school. Well, I went to Jackson Oil and asked them—they had a station there that was coming up for lease, and so I found out how I'd go about it. And they wanted to teach me their way, you know what I mean. Jackson Oil has a certain way of doing things, and they want their jobbers to do the way that should be done. And so that's what I went to school for—I don't know—six weeks. Learn how they wanted their station run. Learn how they wanted things done. You know, the whole thing. This is after I'd been driving. And I don't know, about the time I got ready to take over the station, I just chickened out. I just didn't think I could do it. I didn't think I could stay pinned down to an eight, you know, to an everyday thing doing the same thing and never getting more than fifteen-ten minutes away from the house.

I would say most truck drivers out here are more or less on the loner side. You know, I mean a good operator and that, he'll sit in the truck and he'll do his thing. And you got your cowboys and all that shit out here alright, but I think a good owner/operator is a loner, you know. I mean he can stand his old lady for so long and then he's got to get out. He comes back home, he's a happy man.

In an earlier segment, Dan also talks about how trucking gets "in your blood." Irv, who was described a moment ago as one who regrets not staying with other jobs, elaborates on this theme:

(Why do you think guys keep trucking? Just 'cause it's their business and they know what they're doing and stuff, huh?) Well, did you ever ask a printer—a guy that's worked on a printing press for years—to do some other job? (No, uh uh.) Try it some time. You know what they tell you? They got ink in their blood. They can't get away from it. It's there. It's just something that gets you. You just got to stay with it. Well, trucking is more or less the same way. And once [you] get on a truck and you drive that truck for quite a few years, the hardest thing in the world to do is to get off it. No matter where you go, every time you hear a *putt putt putt* it brings back memories. You see what I mean?

You know, it's a funny thing about the American people. Maybe everybody, maybe human nature. I don't know. You tend to forget the bad things and remember the good things. I mean as far as yourself goes. As far as somebody else goes, you remember the bad things and forget the good things. Did you ever notice that? So if you start to thinking about trucking as an example, you don't think about the times you laid out there in the snow and ice trying to get something going. Or the time you got caught overloaded, you had to pay all your money out for a fine and then borrow money off the company to finish it, and all these kind of things. All you think about is that—hey, that good time you had up there at the truck stop, or that good load of freight you hauled down there, or something like that. You only remember the good things.

Adding to his theory of having it in one's blood, Irv points out that selective memory helps too. Working on the truck in bad weather was mentioned by Cal as a point of pride; for Irv it is something it makes sense to forget. Another reason for continuing is set out by Steve:

But that was how I got into it. And when I got into it, I guess I was expecting a lot more than what I finally realized. Maybe I was looking for a more glamorous occupation or something, but I wasn't in it any time at all and I didn't like it. But I didn't know how to get out of it, because I was paying for a truck, and I figured I'd work my way out of it and hopefully work into something bigger. It's like a second marriage. The triumph of hope over experience. You keep going along hoping that next year it's gonna be better. I don't have a very high opinion of trucking.

Independent trucking is seductive that way. It is easy to get in and then very difficult to keep from getting clobbered. The independent comes up with a down payment on a truck and starts driving, but then has an unpleasant surprise when the checks are lower and the costs higher than he expected (Red describes just such a jolt). Steve says he kept going because he had no choice. But he also talks about "hope"—it will get better eventually. Maybe Irv's theory about natural optimism is right.

Jack uses the "what else could I do this well" tack in discussing the issue:

(Have you thought about doing something else?) Naw, been doing it too damn long. I don't know what I'd—I wouldn't be able to do anything else. I wouldn't be happy, you know. I mean, hey. I mean I wouldn't know how to—I wouldn't be happy doing anything else. I know what I'm doing. I'm good at what I do. And I know I'm good at what I do, and I know how to do it.

There are other discussions of the business in the transcripts. Ike and Jack talk about how they are getting older and now have physical problems that would block them from other jobs. Irv and Will both talk about other jobs they have had where the "confinement" or sense of being "penned up" led them to return to trucking and stay with it. Carl, in an unrecorded conversation, talked about trying a factory job and going crazy with the rigidity of his supervisors. But in all this talking about independent trucking and reasons for staying or not, where is the independence?

Independence Again

Some of the passages on the subject of independence contain direct contradictions. Irv thinks of mechanical work in bad weather as something to forget; Cal thinks of it as requiring the stamina that is cause for pride. Jack thinks being away from home is a negative part of trucking; Dan thinks a man has to get away once in a while. Irv talks about how the value of travel is zero; Will evaluates it highly.

But in other contradictory statements the variations form a pattern. First, independent trucking is seen as negative, in part, because of social labels and business consequences. A trucker is considered a low form of social life; an independent trucker is in a business that returns very little for the amount invested and the personal energy expended. Steve repeats earlier themes from his interview in this judgment of trucking:

> To be perfectly honest, I regret my years in the trucking business. I think that time would have been much better spent, you know, somewhere else, either working for somebody or working for myself in some other kind of business. Because of the hours, and not only the time but the money spent. What kind of return do you got for all that effort and money? I personally think the owner/operator has been grossly underpaid for years, and it's getting worse right now, strange to say.

This evaluation is particularly ironic in view of the popular image of the independent trucker—an admired folkhero making money hand over fist. Favorable social status and wealth *never* appear in the interviews as reasons why independent trucking is a *good* occupation.

There are few positive comments in the general discussions of trucking. There are theories of personal inertia and financial or physical capture—a body in trucking tends to (or has to) stay in trucking. More positive comments emerge when independent trucking is contrasted with other jobs, their own or someone else's.

Ironically the differences sound like "independence," but only in a complicated and interesting way. Independence is, in part, about the lack of *immediate* supervisory control. All the dependencies in the working world have been described in detail. But there is no person, right there, nosing around giving the independent orders all the time. He decides when to roll and when to rest. No one is looking over his shoulder. He does not control the general nature of the work, but he does control the organization of some of the details of its enactment. If everything runs smoothly. As long as he checks in once in a while.

But there is more to independence than this. The independent is in continual motion on a schedule where the usual organization of work into specific times on specific days disappears. In fact, the major characteristic of independence to emerge from these interviews is the distinctiveness, during the trip, of the basic coordinates of experience. While others sleep in their homes or go to the nearby factory or office, he moves through time and space. While he is on a trip the culturally "normal" ways of segmenting time and organizing space no longer apply. Independence comes from a sense of distinctiveness rather than from a sense of control. The independent's world is organized in a distinctive way.

Time and space are two different ways of measuring the same thing—the city is either a hundred some miles or a couple of hours away; the independent thinks in terms of states rather than neighborhoods; regional styles and landscapes shift around him, along with the food and accents in the restaurants; while most people sleep he walks into a buzzing truck stop at 3:00 a.m., wherever he happens to be, and knows that he can have a conversation about a large number of things. The territory in which he is communicatively competent is located everywhere; but it is made up of "stops," not towns or cities. His "news" comes in from the few miles of bubble that moves with him, its size defined by the range of his CB—road conditions, weather, inspection stations, and attractive women in four-wheelers are the reportable events. And on goes the list. I found it disorienting (and then addicting) to be in motion in a time-world where the only thing with a clear beginning and end is the trip itself. It sets a person apart.

Distinctiveness comes in another way too. The truck. It usually has a name, typically feminine. (One truck I saw was named Phredd because the independent's female friend kept complaining about always naming trucks after women.) He owns it. The truck is the obvious focus of the whole experience, the symbol of power, the extension of self into technology under personal control, the American mania for motor vehicles carried to its logical conclusion. I think there is truth in this analysis, or maybe it is just another *Convoy*-prone outsider telling more about himself than about independents.

The elusive but ubiquitous truck. Independents talk about trucks all the time, often to complain about problems with them, but usually in terms of technical detail. My teachers all had a professional concern for appearance and safety, but pointed out that a decked-out chrome-laden tractor, an object of beauty, probably belonged to an independent who was rich before he started or who is about to go out of business. Perhaps the truck is so much just there, part of the water in which they swim, that words are no longer dedicated to its celebration. But there is no getting around it—eighty-thousand pounds of loaded tractor-trailer rolling along the interstate is distinctive.

I know there is more to it than this. After I had tried a bit of driving, independents would often say something like, "it's a thrill, isn't it?" When I described passing another truck on a country road in the one I was driving and said it felt like I had gone into "another dimension," the reaction told me I had said something right. There is more to the truck than independents say, and there is obviously more than I learned. I am reminded of a book on American cowboys that noted that in all the writings about them, outsiders kept forgetting to talk about the horses and cows. Whatever else it represents, the truck must be some part of distinctiveness.

By this reasoning, the opposite of "independent" is "indistinguishable," not "controlled." The shift is more than lexical. As the opposite of "controlled," "independent" means freedom enabled by self-reliance. As the opposite of "indistinguishable," it means noticeable, remarkable. The shift in meaning is from the political to the perceivable, from personal control over what a person does to whether or not he stands out in his social milieu. He can accomplish the latter without having the former. In a standardized, franchised, routinized world that accomplishment is worth something.

The problem comes when outsiders read off the perceivable surface and miss its contradictory depths. Independents tell a lot of stories about post-*Convoy* types who came into independent trucking in pursuit of an image and left shortly after. Tom Corsi (Corsi, Gardner, and Tuck 1982; Corsi and Martin 1982) shows that half of the ICC survey sample of 1977 left their leases by 1980, and that one of the important items correlated with leaving is age/experience. Or, to tie it back into the interviews, Will talks about a couple of new independents: "They did it because of the glamorous stories, but they soon found out how glamorous it is. That glamour had a lot of work to it." The difference between cultural myth and social reality turns cruel when the former attracts the new blood and the latter chews them up and spits them out.

There is one more meaning of "independence" on which to speculate. Independent trucking is a pervasive career. The wife is usually the business half of the team. More than one wife told me that the woman either gets involved in trucking or the marriage breaks up. Driving up to an independent's home, one often sees the truck parked nearby, and much of the time the independent will be around it doing some work. The dining room table is often piled with settlement sheets, record books, quarterly report forms, and whatnot. Tools, parts, and supplies are scattered around, usually in garages, sheds, and basements but sometimes on the kitchen counter. Independent trucker is not something you do; it is something you are. By this reasoning, the opposite of "independent" is not "controlled"; the opposite of "independent" is "alienated."

Independent trucking represents a personal involvement in work that is rare in contemporary America. My guess is that such involvement is generally found among small businesspeople, and like many of them independents may get exhausted, see that the return is not worth the energy, and accept more alienation for more free time. That choice has been talked about a few times in the interviews.

But one must be careful not to get carried away and forget the important role of serendipity and inertia in all the stories. Several stories describe falling into trucking through a chance contact, or because there was no choice, or because it was convenient. The independent talks about staying in trucking because it is what he knows, because he has physical problems, because he does it well, because he cannot afford to get out.

Maybe all this talk about distinctive and unalienated is overdone. But by comparison with most working worlds currently available in the United States, it stands out on those two characteristics. That is a truth. And the discussion helps straighten out why the term "independence" does apply, though not in the way that the cultural image leads outsiders to think it does. Maybe the whole point is to straighten out our image of the independents rather than their reasons for doing what they do. That is what exploration is for, a report on a humanscape rather than an account of why each and every one of its occupants is there.

Chapter 12

Conclusion

Once over Heavily

The working world of the leased independent is one in which he finds himself tangled in webs of dependency. For the most part, he portrays himself in the role of fly rather than spider, his well-being contingent on the intentions of the eight-legged creature who approaches. In chapter after chapter he has described his lack of control. He depends on carriers for freight, for rates, and for the transformation of paperwork into payment. Shippers and customers control loading and unloading, and they can file claims or delay payment by holding up paperwork. Breakdowns leave him vulnerable, often in places where he is a stranger. Federal, state, and local officials can demand a variety of papers and fine him for noncompliance. Some of the papers, like logbooks, are standing jokes; others, like the scrapbook of state documents, are potentially expensive annoyances.

The interviews are rich in patterns of dependency. Even more than that, the dependencies frequently lead to disasters—the outcomes of relationships between independent and other are typically described as negative from the independent's point of view. But throughout the book, when my observations on trips were compared with interview content, the situation was not as bad as the interviews described. Why is the tone so negative?

One answer might be that independents just complain a lot. Independents as well as those who come into contact with them express that opinion. But that is an unacceptable explanatory dodge. One may dismiss problems by attributing their existence to the personality of those who are currently caught up in them, but the pattern of dependency shows up too frequently in interviews, notes, and documents for this explanation to be valid.

Another dodge would be to invoke the representativeness issue.

The group I interviewed are experienced, and most are members of an independent organization. In addition, none of them works among the household goods carriers, an area of the industry that is dominated by leased independents. My teachers were not "random," but then good teachers seldom are. But once again, the patterns are just too strong, too mutually reinforcing, to be dismissed with method quibbles. And the use of the ICC survey and other materials shows that my teachers by and large reflect national statistics.

If those two explanations are inadequate, then why is it that when I asked independent truckers to talk about their careers in any way they chose, the tone was so negative? Is their world *really* that bad? The question is a fundamental one in all forms of human research. What is the relationship between what people say about their worlds and the direct observations of an outsider? One answer centers on the argument about which kind of data—interview or observational—is the "right stuff." But more interesting still is the attitude that both are "right." The more instructive question is to wonder about the relationship between the two types of data.

For the independent trucker interviews, I think the answer lies in the argument that interview content is in service of particular rhetorical goals. The fact of the matter is that leased independents *are* embedded in webs of dependency, and they *are* usually powerless to obtain redress when things go wrong. But it is also a fact that usually the superordinate member of any link in the web does not use his power maliciously. The potential is there, but it is less frequently used than the interviews suggest.

Many of the stories, in a word, represent worst-case scenarios. The reason for that emphasis is that independents made their points more dramatically and effectively by stressing the potential consequences of the situation rather than simply explaining its characteristics. The "worst-case" emphasis is a way of effective teaching, a way to dramatize the texture of a world by emphasizing its danger. The stories and descriptions are true as accounts of dependency but overstated in terms of frequency of negative outcome of events due to that dependency. But they do make the point.

Dependence

Frequency of disastrous outcomes is one thing, but the emphasis on dependency is another. Why didn't the independents talk more about positive characteristics of their work, like distinctiveness? The dependency theme is a pattern that recurs in several different problem areas; but the problems center on just those areas where the cultural image and the social reality contradict. Independents are caught in a sociocultural squeeze play; their image is used to celebrate traditional American values that their working world contradicts. When they talk in informal interviews, many of the stories highlight those parts of their working world that generate the contradictions.

Traditional American independence centers on personal freedom. The notion has several correlates. In space it means you are in motion; in time you do what you want when you please; socially you have no enduring ties; economically you are an individual entrepreneur. Since you have freedom in all these domains, it follows that no one is around with control over you. Finally, all this is enabled by your competence; you are independent in part because you are self-sufficient.

The typical situation of the contemporary American worker is different. You are settled in a mortgaged home, probably with a family. You work in a nine to five (or at least regularly scheduled) job. You are part of a community with a stable group of friends and acquaintances. You receive a salary for your specialized work as part of a large company. You take orders from your supervisor. Though you may have some skills, these are now known as "hobbies." For the most part you rely on retail and service outlets for your needs.

Assume, for current purposes, that the two ideal types are reasonable descriptions of cultural models. The former is associated with the American past and the latter with the present. The former is highly valued, the image personified by the cowboy and more recently by the independent trucker. The latter is the life of "quiet desperation" portrayed tragically in plays like *Death of a Salesman*, in films like *Blue Collar* and *Ordinary People*.

Social, cultural, and economic change since the Civil War has reduced most of the means of economic survival that allow one to fulfill the traditional national ideal, yet it is still honored as a worthy goal. Independent trucking becomes a particularly cruel tease, because it holds out the surface appearances of the ideal, but then with time and experience it stresses (and sometimes economically ruins) those who step into the role with the contradictions.

You do move in space, though you had better have your state permits in order. You do, to some extent, organize your own schedule, though waiting time and deadheading and late delivery claims can be devastating. You do work alone, unless you are one member of a sleeper team. You are hardly an individual entrepreneur, since your access to freight and the rates by which you are paid are not in your control. While no immediate supervisor hovers behind your back, you are to some extent subject to the whims of your dispatcher, and you usually call in regularly with status reports on the trip. You may be a reasonably competent mechanic, but many of the problems with tractor and trailer are simply beyond your ability to handle.

One independent joked that you would have to have a second trailer carrying everything you needed to keep things in shape. Though the independent usually works alone, the "social loner" image must be qualified by the dedication to family that many express.

The point is simply that independent trucking falls into the sociocultural cracks. As a working world, it has attributes of the cultural image, but it is also heavily laced with the more typical social patterns of contemporary American occupations. Much of the interviews express that conflict. When independents talk about their work, what they say creates a pattern, best described as betrayal of the cultural myth by the contemporary reality of their working world. Independent truckers are the last of the cowboys, but at the moment they are trying to figure out how to get around all that barbed wire. The open-range cowboy was lucky; he was gone before the image-making started. The independent truckers have to live with image and reality at the same time.

Deregulation and Independents

Until recently, transportation was a regulated market. In the current era, a policy switch has been thrown and the trend is "deregulation." Among the arguments for deregulation are improved service and reduced prices through competition in a free market. In fact, rates are dropping, and industry publications are full of feature articles on the importance of marketing.

At first glance, deregulation looks like a partial solution to the problems of dependency that independents described in their interviews. But so far deregulation has hurt leased independents rather than helping them. In my observations and conversations with truckers over the last two years, it has been interesting (but not particularly pleasant) to watch their attitudes change. Initially they wanted to help deregulation eliminate the barriers that hindered their access to the marketplace. Now they criticize deregulation, because its negative consequences have been twofold:

1) Rates have declined. As leased independents, they absorb 72 percent to 75 percent of the cut if they have their own trailer. Furthermore, declining rates place increased pressures on carriers to "flat-rate" loads. In other words, the carrier offers the independent a fixed fee rather than a percentage of the revenue he charges. The fee is lower than the percentage would be, so the carrier can retain more of the revenue. There are stories in the interviews and in conversations about the increasing practice of flat-rating, particularly on trip-leased loads going back home.

2) ICC regulations and enforcement capabilities that benefit leased independents have been reduced. Cutbacks in personnel in the ICC

office that handles independents' problems have now rendered them ineffective in enforcing regulations, except for a few cases of particularly unethical carriers about whom many independents complain. In addition, independents see the ICC regulations designed to benefit them—like fuel compensation and private carrier leasing—rejected by or tied up in the courts.

Deregulation, in short, has given the independent lower revenue and less protection from the ICC. In contrast, the benefits of deregulation—eased entry—are difficult for an independent to implement. First of all, rates decline and operating costs increase. Rate competition in the deregulated marketplace will reward large carriers who can take advantage of operating efficiencies that come with size. Second, if he intends to operate interstate, an independent must deal with each state on matters of registration, authority, fuel permits, and the increasing number of weight/distance/axle taxes. For the independent, the burdens in terms of paperwork, costs, and posted bonds is overwhelming. He lacks the leverage of larger carriers in dealing with the many jurisdictions in which they operate. Third, unless he has established relationships with shippers in an area, the lone independent is at a competitive disadvantage in finding loads. Large carriers have established reputations that often lead shippers to choose them over an unknown.

In short, the experience of "deregulation" has created, among the independents I have worked with, a sense of frustration and betrayal. To date they have absorbed many of the costs of deregulation, like reduced rates, but have not been able to take advantage of many of its benefits, like increased business opportunities. Even if private carriage leasing opens up, indications are that they will enter the same kind of controlled relationship as they currently are in with the for-hire carriers.

At the moment at least two possible futures would allow for the lease-free life in the world of regulated freight. One way would involve true deregulation, setting the independents free from all but safety regulations. They would still have neither the advantage of economics of scale nor any leverage with the states. But this option would allow them to roam the marketplace, establish relationships and reputations with particular shippers, and compete in terms of service and rates. At present this option does not exist. Only time will tell if it does come about, and if it does, only more time will tell how independents will fare in a completely deregulated trucking market.

The other possibility would be for independents to take the current situation on its own terms and establish worker-owned businesses. In a way, this would be a return to the early days of trucking when most motor carriers were individuals driving their own trucks. In this scenario, an independent would own and operate his own truck, and he would also own and operate a part of his own carrier. This would yield the advantages of scale and leverage while allowing him to retain his distinctiveness and obtain more control. It would be difficult, however, to organize a group committed to the idea of personal distinctiveness, as the recent history of independent trucker politics demonstrates, but it is another possible future under deregulation.

At the present, though, the independent trucker sees deregulation as a hoax. If anything, the experience of declining rates and the encounters with state jurisdictions among those trying to implement their own authority have only amplified and made explicit the conflict between independence and control, while contributing almost nothing to its resolution.

Even if the independents are eventually cut loose, life would not be easy. Large trucking companies get "fleet discounts" on everything from the purchase of trucks through maintenance and insurance up to and including fuel purchases at the truck stop. In a world where much of the rhetoric of business requires an "institutional" rather than an individual identity, carriers can deal more effectively with federal and state agencies, maintain the relationships with attorneys to redress grievances, hire the accountants who maintain the records, and obtain the employee benefits that they require.

The individual independent, in contrast, has neither the scale nor the institutional identity to exert any leverage in the situations that make up his working world. In the preinflationary days of the 1960s and early 1970s, he made a living by working in the lower rated niches of the trucking industry. Inflation, especially in the price of fuel, changed all that. Rates, over which he had no control, held steady and then began to drop as deregulation moved in. At the same time, benefits of deregulation targeted at independents came to little.

The free market, if it actually comes about, will reward economic efficiency. But when independents talk about their working world, profitability is not what they emphasize, except to note its absence. They obtain a distinctiveness and an involvement in their work, things that are simply not very attainable in the usual working roles available to them. They are not making a good living now; many have gone out of business. With the free market pressure toward efficiencies of scale, they will become even less competitive.

Steve said that independent truckers are like dinosaurs. Many little animals are picking away at them; before the information from all the different sites gets to the dinosaur's brain, it will be dead.

On the other hand, some independents like Will are more guarded, saying only that they hope to be a survivor, hope that things will get better. So do I. But at the moment it looks like the only way they will survive is either to get organized or join one of the few carriers with huge independent fleets now appearing under deregulation. In either case, the meaning of the "independence" in "independent trucker" will become even more complicated.

Toward a Comparative Future

Independents Declared is a case study, a portrait of a humanscape depicting its internal terrain and its location in a broader cultural region. Case studies can be placed in broader theoretical regions as well. By and large I have neglected this placement, though there are a variety of theoretical frameworks into which the case fits—economic theory, organization theory, not to mention the classic social theories of Marx, Weber, and Durkheim.

Anthropology constructs theory through comparison. In this study, the comparison is within and between individuals who work as independent truckers, an appropriate level for the goal of investigating a single occupational role. Eventually, comparisons can be conducted with other ethnographies of the role, with ethnographies of other roles in American society, and with ethnographies of similar and different roles in other cultures. While these higher level comparisons are not on the agenda for now, I would like to use a couple of examples to show their promise.

I found no other ethnographies of independent truckers. The best known book-length treatments in the professional transportation literature are the works of Wyckoff and Maister, cited earlier. They are, for the most part, based on surveys supplemented with archival work. The popular literature sampled in the last chapter is of course written to entertain and to celebrate American myths, not to investigate the actual working world of anybody.

Some books lie between the popular and the professional literature. One, *Trucker* by Jane Stern (1975), is a book of photographs and short texts that suggests the *Convoy* view of trucking. The work is superficial and lacking in detail. A more serious effort is Axel Madsen's *Open Road* (1982). He covers many of the important technical and regulatory details in an entertaining prose style. He also weaves in a fictitious story about an older man and younger woman team who mostly go out and experience the "war stories" that the popular literature celebrates. He adopts the "cover everything" strategy, so a chapter on a national tractor drag race is prominently featured, for example. Also missing from the trucking literature are ethnographies of company drivers, a need that must be filled if we are to clearly understand the differences and similarities between them and independents.

To find proper ethnographic studies requires broadening the comparison to occupational roles that resemble independents'. A close relative and occasional antagonist of trucking, historically and occupationally, is the railroad. Frederick C. Gamst, in his book *The Hogshead: An Industrial Ethnology of the Locomotive Engineer* (1980), looked at occupational roles in a way similar to mine. He had the advantage of more than six years and two thousand trips as a "railroad employee in engine service" before he became an ethnographer, a past that adds background knowledge to his study that I cannot begin to approach.

Perhaps because of his backround, Gamst emphasizes the subtle and intricate relationships among the details of regulation, technology, and conditions as they enter into the management of actual trips. I could not match his expertise without several years' work in the trucking industry. Such a parallel account would be possible, though. I talked with an analytically minded independent in California a few times. At one point he gave an example of the sort of "stream of consciousness" thinking he does sometimes on trips, scanning the gauges, the traffic, the kinds of freight moving in different directions on the highway, and sensing the state of his truck from its "feel." His account had the flavor of some of the passages in Gamst's book.

But in this study I left out discussions of many of the technical details. To understand why, consider a simple example or two from the panel of gauges in the cab. There is a "pyrometer" that measures the temperature of exhaust gases at the manifold. There is an "ap gauge" ("ap" is short for "application") that shows the amount of air pressure going to the braking system. Or consider the variety of transmissions, some of them involving the stick plus two switches for "high/low range" and "direct/overdrive." Just an account of the technology in the cab would require much space and technical detail. My strategy was to produce those descriptions only when interview passages or observations required them.

In spite of our different approaches, though, some similarities emerge. The pervasiveness of regulations in the role comes through in both accounts. Gamst's opening sketch of getting ready for a trip (4–12) and much of his chapters four, five, and six are descriptions of the role of regulatory information in the organization of the details of work. He notes the temporal distinctiveness of railroading (28–30) as well as other characteristics reminiscent of passages quoted earlier, like opportunities to use one's own judgment and the need to flexibly adapt in sophisticated ways to unforeseen circumstances.

He also briefly notes the family-oriented nature of most of the "rails" and the stress created for wives and children (110–13).

Differences also emerge. Rails work in crews, where independents typically work alone. Rails are union employees operating company equipment, where independents are usually nonunion and operate their own equipment. Most striking is the difference in training. Rails enter into long-term apprenticeships (now often involving technical schooling as well) before they are fully established as engineers. Required training for truckers is far less extensive, to put it mildly. In fact, there is currently some controversy in the trucking industry about the quality of both private and company-affiliated training programs.

Another related occupational role, one that has attracted a substantial amount of attention in anthropology, is that of fishermen. Mark Miller, for one, has written on the relationship between regulatory policy and the actual details of work (Miller and Van Maanen 1979). He writes elsewhere of the ongoing "rationalization" of the role, the importance of converting from a romantic identity to one learned and implemented in terms of standard business practices (Van Maanen, Miller, and Johnson 1982). That discussion is reminiscent of some of the passages quoted in this book; it was a theme of the Small Business Administration course I attended. No more living from trip to trip with your filing cabinet in your shirt pocket, as Red once put it. The independent who survives now must be a good businessman.

A book-length study of fishermen is Michael Orbach's *Hunters, Seamen, and Entrepreneurs* (1977), an ethnographic account of the tuna seinermen of San Diego. Some of the same issues come to life in his book, but he provides more detail on social interaction among the crews, on making decisions to organize the work, and on the relationship between work and community life. The latter emphasis was facilitated because many of the Italian and Portuguese fishermen also shared ethnic urban neighborhoods on shore.

The studies for comparisons within the United States are now available and growing in number. Future work with small farmers and other small businesses will add even more information. Comparison across cultures will be equally interesting. Gamst has already initiated the trend with his study of railroading in Ethiopia. Some of the independent trade publications, like *Owner-Operator* and *Overdrive* occasionally feature letters or articles about independent trucking in other countries. A study in Germany (Gutmann 1981) and recent newspaper reports of an independent trucker shutdown in France are also suggestive of productive future comparative work.

This book stands as an investigation of an occupational role, but

I hope it will become part of the process of cross-group and cross-cultural comparison. Such comparisons, as I hope the above examples suggest, serve as methodological checks. Areas that were neglected or emphasized in one study stand out when compared to others. But even more interesting, the comparisons will lead us to a richer understanding of the relationship between people and their occupations in our own society and in others. They will become part of the recent growth of the new anthropology of work (Gamst 1981; Wallman 1979) and the more venerable anthropology of industry (Holzberg and Giovannini 1981).

Many people (including some anthropologists) think of cultural anthropology as the study of certain kinds of people. The history of the field gives reasonable grounds for that confusion. But it is a confusion, for anthropology is a unique *way* to study *any* kind of people. Theory and method must shift to accommodate the different characteristics of the way nontraditional people live. But at its core the basic research style remains the same—find teachers, spend time in their world, and struggle with the problem of figuring out a systematic way to tell others what has been learned.

Comparison of humanscapes will highlight the general truths of life in contemporary American society. Comparison within other modern states will be equally revealing of work and life in other parts of the world. Comparison of those comparisons will produce still higher level truths about contemporary life. That sort of theory is the most useful imaginable, with its rich yields of that elusive quality called "perspective" and its guidelines for an approach to problems based on good information rather than preconceived notions. It's a load of freight worth delivering.

Appendix I

Analyzing
Interviews

The career history interview is a format designed to let the interviewee have control. The researcher presents the general topic and requests clarification or detail in areas already selected as significant by the interviewee. The general idea is to let the interviewee run where he will, speaking about whatever comes to mind in whatever way he chooses. If you just let people talk about their world, the reasoning goes, themes will emerge that indicate its perceived texture.

To work with this kind of material, transcripts are necessary; their preparation is tedious work, since a clean hour of talk might take six to eight hours to transcribe. I transcribed the first two interviews but then used the help of Roberta Albers at the University of Maryland. Transcription was done on a word-processor to facilitate "proof-listening"—going over the transcript, listening to the tape, and checking for errors.

The next step was the reduction of transcribed interviews to manageable chunks for analysis. The details are described in Agar and Hobbs (1983), but the general procedure is to divide an interview into segments by marking off major breaks in content. Sometimes the breaks are difficult to find, but surgical precision is not necessary. Each segment is numbered: in the five hundred double-spaced pages of transcript that underlie this book, there are a total of 403 segments.

Counting up the segments, 58 percent of them were accounted for by the analysis in this book. (By accounted for, I mean they were either directly quoted or referred to in the text, although the quote or reference may not cover everything in the segment.) Twelve percent were eliminated because they dealt with things going on around the interview rather than with the interview content. Nineteen percent were eliminated because they dealt with topics irrelevant to this study. Only 11 percent remained unaccounted for. Looking at the amount of the transcript rather than number of segments, the percentage of eliminated material drops to 5 percent, since these segments were typically short. The neglected topics stay the same, and the unaccounted for material drops to 10 percent. The material included in the analysis rises to 66 percent. When you find a pattern that draws from that much material—not to mention notes and other data—you know that the pattern is significant.

1985
Update

The trucking industry is very much in motion. The most intensive research for this book—the interviews and the trips—spanned about a year, from October 1981, to July 1982. The analysis and writing occupied the next year, ending in late 1983. In just those few years the industry has changed. The Motor Carrier Act of 1980 began an ongoing process of deregulation that met the recession/depression of the early 1980s head on. It is not yet clear, nor will it be for some time, what the future trucking industry will look like or what the independents' roles in it will be. Some trends can be described, though, particularly those related to interview passages quoted earlier.

In the first chapter, "private carriers" were described—those shippers that maintain trucks driven by company employees to carry their own goods. They do not have to deal with the ICC. At the time of my research, independents were not allowed to work for them. In February of 1982, the ICC announced a new rule—independents could begin to work in "private carriage." The decision was immediately taken to court by the for-hire carriers, and there it stayed for quite some time. The April 9, 1984, *Transport Topics* (a weekly industry newspaper published by the American Trucking Associations) reported that the Supreme Court refused to hear the final appeal, so the decision now stands.

On April 30, *Transport Topics* set out guidelines for private carrier leasing. The private carriage lease includes the same old thirty-day minimum and the requirements for insurance, permitting, and cargo damage responsibilities that are required in leases with for-hire carriers. It is too early to tell what kind of opportunity private carrier leasing will be. However, independents now have a new market in which to offer their services, a substantial one given the earlier statistics showing that most trucks on the road are pulling for private carriers. But the relationship will have the same dependency characteristics described in this study. And private carriage is not regulated by the ICC, so an independent will not be able to get any help there. With rates as low as they are right now, private carriers will hesitate to take on the expenses of transportation management and payment to independents when they can ship their goods with for-hire carriers at lower cost.

One hopeful sign on the horizon lies in the old economic laws of supply and demand. The supply of independents is down and demand is up. Supply is down because so many were forced out of business by prolonged inflation followed by deregulation and recession. For the same reasons, demand increased as more carriers shifted to leased trucks to lower their operating costs and avoid unionization and other problems of employee management. Consider this quote from a *Transport Topics* report on a panel at the American Trucking Associations Sales and Marketing Council (the panelists are three carrier presidents):

> Mr. Long said this supply-and-demand situation will require changes in the packages carriers offer owner-operators. Mr. Tyler suggested that carriers will have to market and sell themselves to owner-operators, recruiting and retaining them as they do shipper customers. Mr. Shertz said dealing with owner-operators is still a matter of negotiation and expressed confidence that carriers can do more to treat owner-operators as businessmen (April 9, 1984, 4).

The remarks reinforce what I hear at the Maryland independent organization meetings, as well as my experience presenting a paper based on this book at the Transportation Research Forum meetings in November 1983. I did not know what kind of response to expect from the mixed group of private and public sector and academic audiences. I was surprised to find the strongest interest come from the carriers who use independents. I eventually learned that the reason was increased demand and reduced supply. "Who are those people and how do we recruit and retain the good ones?" was the question of interest, an interest motivated by their cost savings in leasing rather than employing drivers and maintaining fleets.

As long as the demand holds, the policy changes that enlarge the markets in which independents offer their services offer the most optimistic sign. (Other recent policy changes concerning the trip-lease, not detailed in this update, also fit this trend.) In the long run, if supply increases and the amount of freight moved around the country by truck declines as America shifts from a manufacturing to a service economy, opportunities for independents could decline again. And the large carriers that are buying up more and more of the market may opt for nonunion company fleets in the future. Right now, though, carriers continue to lower the rates and look for independents to haul the cheap freight and absorb the operating costs. The paradox is striking.

In late 1984 a truck safety bill became federal law. The American Automobile Association worked for, and eventually won, a ban on heavy truck traffic on the beltway around Washington, D.C. Truckers, independent and carrier alike, now talk about their negative public image on issues of safety. The independents I see regularly at meetings of the Maryland organization link some of the safety problems to deregulation. With the severe competition in trucking, rates are driven too low. Independents have to push harder, drive longer, and spend less on maintenance. Carriers with company fleets have to drop driver wages to the point where the quality declines. Well-intentioned legislators always carefully distinguish between economic and safety regulations. The distinction only works at a distance.

In general, the trucking industry feels that its problems are not adequately understood by the public. And the public, known as "four-wheelers" when they are on the interstate, are not particularly loved by independents. There are segments in the interviews that deal with the topic. Four-wheelers are incompetent drivers. They don't understand that trucks can't accelerate and decelerate like cars. They don't know that the truck's maneuverability is limited. They don't realize that an accident involving a truck, which is usually spectacular because of its size, is often the fault of a four-wheeler. Four-wheelers are not crazy about trucks, either. They complain about speed, about highway damage, and about accidents.

On trips during my research, we seldom drove at fifty-five miles per hour, but we almost never exceeded sixty-five to seventy miles per hour. A tractor cannot run at high speed too long without bringing on a mechanical disaster. The justification for speed, of course, is profit. The faster you cover the territory, the more money you're making. The speeds I witnessed usually fit the ambient speed on the interstates, but trucks are expected or required to stay in the right lane. A lackadaisical four-wheeler in front of you and uncooperative traffic on your left are an added expense. Of the seven different independents I traveled with, one was sometimes a road bully who put his lights in the rear window of a car and stayed there until it got out of the way. The other six muttered or cussed, but waited at a safe distance until they could get around in some reasonable way.

Then there is the issue of highway damage. The Department of Transportation recently completed a study, a controversial one that I can't begin to cover here. But the trucking industry attacked the study for several reasons. The design life of the interstate system was twenty years, and the fact that the system is now in need of repair is no surprise, particularly since state cutbacks led to scrimping on maintenance. Several parts of the system were not built well—a favorite example is the Baltimore-Washington Parkway, restricted only to cars, which is falling apart more quickly than many nearby stretches of heavily traveled interstate. Once again, truckers argue that they are being held financially responsible for damage that is not entirely their fault.

Red recently returned from a panel on accidents saying that no one ever got around to talking about causes. A recent study commissioned by the DOT found that "although accidents involving large trucks were less likely to occur than accidents involving passenger cars, the consequences of large-truck accidents were much more severe" (Eicher et al. 1982:vii). Three-fourths of large truck accidents involved another vehicle, three-quarters of those, a passenger car. The same study noted that data were inadequate for "complete causation analysis" (p. V-6); in other words, the study did not test the frequent trucker's complaint that accidents are usually the four-wheeler's fault. Another public complaint—about the new "monster" trucks with twin trailer—also irritates independents and others in the trucking industry. They argue that the new width only allows trucks to be as wide as intercity buses; the western states that have allowed twin trailers for years show no difference in accident rates with single unit trailers.

I don't mean to belittle important arguments that truck driver training is often inadequate, that safety inspections reveal many problems with such critical mechanical components as the braking system, or that current economic pressures can lead to skimpiness in maintenance. Nor do I mean to say that trucks don't damage highways or that some drivers (trucker and four-wheeler) shouldn't be driving. But after a couple of years inside the trucking industry, you begin to understand the indpendents' feelings that some unpleasant truths about trucks are blown out of proportion. There is more to the issues than most four-wheelers realize.

Other regulatory changes have occurred. In July 1984 the president signed the Surface Transportation Assistance Act (STAA). The yearly federal highway use tax went from $210 per year to $550, and the tax on diesel fuel increased six cents per gallon. Running a hundred thousand miles per year at five miles per gallon results in a total tax of $1,750, a $1,540 per year increase. In order to give independents a break, the law specifies that owners of five or fewer trucks are exempt from the increase the first year.

The positive side of the STAA is that it requires states to standardize length and weight rules. The independent can run his eighty thousand pounds and forty-eight foot trailer with any length tractor in any state of the union. The STAA also allows twin trailers, a reform that does not matter much to independents, since they usually carry freight that reaches eighty thousand pounds too quickly to take advantage of the added capacity.

The positive side is tempered, however, by a new form of state-by-state problem. Exit length and weight; enter the problem of the application of standardization to particular roads. As a federal law, the STAA can require standardization only on interstates and some federally funded primary routes. Which routes? And what about "access"? The independent has to go where the load is and to where the load is going. He has to leave the highway for fuel, food, rest, repairs, and the company terminal.

A list of routes was released by the Federal Highway Administration (FHWA) (April 11, 1983—dates refer to *Transport Topics* reports). Court challenges quickly followed in four states and modifications were issued in nine others (May 2, 1983). Connecticut refused to allow twin trailers (May 23, 1983), but lost its case in court (February 27, 1984). Department of Transportation Secretary Dole "attributed much of the designated route controversy to the failure by some states to provide a reasonable network of primary routes to supplement Interstate System operations of twin trailer units" (May 23, 1983). An FHWA official noted that "the issue of designating routes for longer and wider trucks could take a few years to resolve completely . . ." (August 1, 1983). A final route designation was proposed (September 19, 1983), but the proposals "allow the states to establish individual reasonable access provisions." Another lawsuit was filed challenging the designated route system by an auto consumer group. In August a group of trucking industries filed a suit that the allowed highways were too limited. Finally, the truck safety bill signed into law at the end of 1984 specified the roads to which the new rules applied as a matter of federal law. But as recently as August 1985 the American Trucking Associations complained to the DOT that access rules were not being enforced. Several states were hindering interstate trucks.

Another problem with the states, one mentioned occasionally in the quoted interviews, involves state taxes. The following sample of *Transport Topics* items shows the increases. For a tractor-trailer registered for eighty thousand pounds, Virginia's license fee went from $960 to $1,200. Maryland's fuel permit fee went from $3 to $25. Pennsylvania passed a new axle tax of $36, for a total of $180 for a five-axle tractor-trailer (that tax is now in court). Arkansas passed a new tax of $175 or 5 cents per mile. Kentucky passed a new tax of 2.85 cents per mile for trucks registered above sixty thousand pounds. Illinois raised its tax on diesel fuel from 7.5 cents to 13.5 cents. New Jersey increased its permit fee from $6 to $25; New York from $5 to $15. Indiana diesel fuel tax increased 3.9 cents per gallon with an 8-cent surcharge for motor carriers. This list is representative but incomplete. It does not include a discussion of "retaliation," a state adding on a tax only on the trucks from those states that have passed new taxes that affect its own trucks. For example, *Transport Topics* reports that Georgia retaliated against both Pennsylvania and Kentucky trucks with new taxes (November 21, 1983). Maine scheduled retaliation taxes against twelve other states (December 10, 1984), and a private carrier group sued Florida because of retaliation (February 18, 1985).

Independents in particular, and the trucking industry in general, now see themselves engaged in a fight against a state feeding frenzy in increasing and new truck taxes. The states of course justify increasing taxes by citing rising costs of highway maintenance and declining tax revenues. But the moral of the state taxes and the federal highway access problem is clear; interstate trucking will probably always fall into the cracks on some issues of state-federal authority. The new truck safety law is now under discussion, and in part it aims to standardize safety inspections, taxing, and permitting. In the next few years such issues will provide another laboratory to test the prediction.

There are other changes to discuss—changes in the economy, in the industry, and in the regulatory agencies. But this is only an update, not another book. The independents' situation in leasing on to for-hire carriers could improve as they find themselves in a seller's market. But federal and state fees spiral upward and rates have declined. And the latest crisis, insurance costs, has inspired a call for an ICC investigation (August 26, 1985). *Transport Topics* reports that three hundred to four hundred percent increases in insurance payments are now common. The changes reported in this update particularly affect the small-scale independent who does not have the leverage or economies of scale of the large carrier. The independents' future does not look promising, but I have to agree with the industry trade publications—it is still not clear how all this is going to work out. So far, though, nothing has changed that alters the basic conclusion of this book—independent truckers personify an American contradiction. They aspire to fulfill the mythic American past of individual self-reliance in a contemporary world that won't allow it. It's an impossible job.

Literature Cited

Agar, Michael. 1983. "Political Talk: Thematic Analysis of a Policy Argument." *Policy Studies Review* 2: 601–14.

Agar, Michael H., and Jerry R. Hobbs. 1983. "Natural Plans: Using AI Planning in the Analysis of Ethnographic Interviews." *Ethos* 11:33-48.

American Trucking Associations, Inc. 1983. *Federal Motor Carrier Safety Regulations (Parts 390-399)*. Washington, D.C.: ATA, Inc.

Anderson, Richard. 1979. "Maps and Trailers: A Restudy." In *Ethnolinguistics: Boas, Sapir and Whorf Revisited*, edited by Madeleine Mathiot. The Hague: Mouton.

Brill, Steven. 1978. *The Teamsters*. New York: Pocket Books.

Broehl, Wayne G. 1954. *Trucks, Trouble and Triumph: The Norwalk Truck Line Company*. New York: Prentice-Hall.

Corsi, Thomas M. 1979. "The Impact of Multiple-Unit Fleet Owners in the Owner-Operator Segment on Regulatory Reform." *Transportation Journal* 19: 44–59.

Corsi, Thomas M., and John C. Martin. 1982. "An Explanatory Model of Turnover among Owner-Operators." *Journal of Business Logistics* 3: 47–71.

Corsi, Thomas M., Leland L. Gardner, and J. Michael Tuck. 1982. "Owner-Operators and the Motor Carrier Act of 1980." *Logistics and Transportation Review* 18: 225–78.

Crouch, Cleo. 1975. *My Life on the Road*. Hicksville N.Y.: Exposition Press.

De Felice, A.R., et al. 1937. "Progress in the Regulation of Motor Carriers by the Interstate Commerce Commission." *George Washington Law Review* 5: 791–808.

Department of Transportation. 1981. *Options for Uniform State Regulations*. Working Paper No. 1, in coordination with the ICC.

Eicher, J.P., H.D. Robertson, and G.R. Toth. 1982. *Large Truck Accident Causation. (Report # DOT HS-806-300)*. Springfield, Va.: National Technical Information Service.

Fellmeth, Robert C. 1970. *The Interstate Commerce Omission*. New York: Grossman.

Filgas, James F. 1967. *Yellow in Motion: A History of Yellow Transit Freight Lines, Incorporated*. Bloomington: Bureau of Business Research.

Franklin, Max. 1977. *The Last of the Cowboys*. New York: Signet.

Gamst, Frederick C. 1980. *The Hogshead: An Industrial Ethnology of the Locomotive Engineer*. New York: Holt Rinehart and Winston.

———. 1981. "Considerations for an Anthropology of Work." *Anthropology of Work Newsletter* 2(1):7–9.

Gutmann, M.G. 1981. *The Working Conditions of Professional Drivers: Effects on Productivity and Road Safety*. Paris: European Conference of Ministers of Transport.

Holzberg, Carol S., and Maureen J. Giovannini. 1981. "Anthropology and Industry: Reappraisal and New Directions." *Annual Review of Anthropology* 10: 317–60.

Interstate Commerce Commission. 1952. *ICC Reports, Motor Carrier Cases* 52: 675–748.

———. 1958. *ICC Reports, Motor Carrier Cases* 68: 553–65.

———. 1978. *The Independent Trucker: Nationwide Survey of Owner-Operators*. Washington, D.C.: ICC Bureau of Economics.

———. 1979. *The Independent Trucker: Follow-up Survey of Owner-Operators*. Washington, D.C.: ICC Office of Policy and Analysis.

Karolevitz, Robert F. 1966. *This Was Trucking: A Pictorial History of the First Quarter Century of Commercial Motor Vehicles*. Seattle: Superior Publishing Co.

Madsen, Axel. 1982. *Open Road: Truckin' on the Biting Edge*. San Diego: Harcourt Brace Jovanovich.

Maister, David H. 1980. *Management of Owner-Operator Fleets*. Lexington, Mass.: Lexington Books.

Miller, Marc L., and John Van Maanen. 1979. "Boats Don't Fish. People Do: Some Ethnographic Notes on the Federal Management of Fisheries in Gloucester." *Human Organization* 38: 377–85.

Norton, B.W.L. 1978. *Convoy*. New York: Dell.

Office of Defense Transportation. 1946. *Civilian War Transport: 1941–1946*. Washington, D.C.: Government Printing Office.

Orbach, Michael K. 1977. *Hunters, Seamen, and Entrepreneurs: The Tuna Seinermen of San Diego*. Berkeley: University of California Press.

Russell, P.J. 1971. *The Motor Wagons: The Origin and History of Long-Distance Truck Transportation*. Akron: Pioneer Motor Traffic Club of Akron.

Starr, Edward A. 1945. *From Trail Dust to Star Dust*. Dallas: Transportation Press.

Stern, Jane. 1975. *Trucker: A Portrait of the Last American Cowboy.* New York: McGraw-Hill.

Taff, Charles. 1975. *Commercial Motor Transportation.* Cambridge, Md.: Cornell Maritime Press.

Taylor, Lonn. 1983a. "The Open-Range Cowboy of the Nineteenth Century." In Lonn Taylor and Ingrid Maar, eds., *The American Cowboy.* Washington, D.C.: American Folklife Center, Library of Congress.

———.1983b. "The Cowboy Hero: An American Myth Examined." In Lonn Taylor and Ingrid Maar, eds., *The American Cowboy.* Washington, D.C.: American Folklife Center, Library of Congress.

Taylor, Lonn, and Ingrid Maar, eds. 1983. *The American Cowboy.* Washington, D.C.: American Folklife Center, Library of Congress.

Thomas, James H. 1979. *Long Haul: Truckers, Truck Stops and Trucking.* Memphis: Memphis State University Press.

U.S. Congress. Senate. Committee on Interstate and Foreign Commerce. 1955. *Trip Leasing. Hearings on S. 898.*

———. 1956. *Trip Leasing. Hearings on H.R. 6973 and S. 898.*

Van Maanen, John, Marc L. Miller, and Jeffrey C. Johnson. 1982. "An Occupation in Transition: Traditional and Modern Forms of Commercial Fishing." *Sociology of Work and Occupations* 9: 193–216.

Wallman, Susan. 1979. *Social Anthropology of Work.* New York: Academic Press.

Wyckoff, D. Daryl. 1979. *Truck Drivers in America.* Lexington, Mass.: Lexington Books.

Wyckoff, D. Daryl, and David H. Maister. 1975. *The Owner-Operator: Independent Trucker.* Lexington, Mass.: Lexington Books.

Index

Transportation Research Forum,
16, 181
Trip-leasing, 45-46, 47, 48, 50, 52,
58-65, 171, 181
Trucker, 174
Trucks (*See* Tractor-trailers)
Truck stops, 39-40, 66

Unions, 21, 56, 91-97, 126

Weight limits (*See* Regulation)
Wife's role, 17, 36, 69, 128-29,
156-57, 166, 171
Women truckers, 17